# IN JESUS' NAME

## 5 ALTARS OF PRAYER
### THAT MOVE HEAVEN AND EARTH

RICK DUBOSE

**Chosen**
*a division of Baker Publishing Group*
Minneapolis, Minnesota

© 2023 by Richard W. DuBose

Published by Chosen Books
Minneapolis, Minnesota
www.chosenbooks.com

Chosen Books is a division of
Baker Publishing Group, Grand Rapids, Michigan

Printed in the United States of America

Library of Congress Cataloging-in-Publication Data
Names: DuBose, Rick, 1957– author.
Title: In Jesus' name : 5 altars of prayer that move heaven and earth / Rick DuBose.
Description: Minneapolis, Minnesota : Chosen Books, a division of Baker
    Publishing Group, [2023] | Includes bibliographical references.
Identifiers: LCCN 2023000034 | ISBN 9780800763657 (trade paper) | ISBN
    9780800763671 (casebound) | ISBN 9781493443970 (ebook)
Subjects: LCSH: Prayer—Pentecostal churches.
Classification: LCC BV227 .D83 2023 | DDC 248.3/2—dc23/eng/20230413
LC record available at https://lccn.loc.gov/2023000034

Unless otherwise indicated, Scripture quotations are from THE HOLY BIBLE, NEW INTERNATIONAL VERSION®, NIV® Copyright © 1973, 1978, 1984, 2011 by Biblica, Inc.® Used by permission. All rights reserved worldwide.

Scripture quotations identified ESV are from The Holy Bible, English Standard Version® (ESV®), copyright © 2001 by Crossway, a publishing ministry of Good News Publishers. Used by permission. All rights reserved. ESV Text Edition: 2016

Cover design by Rob Williams, InsideOut Creative Arts, Inc.

Baker Publishing Group publications use paper produced from sustainable forestry practices and post-consumer waste whenever possible.

23  24  25  26  27  28  29     7  6  5  4  3  2  1

# CONTENTS

# FOREWORD

Growing up in a Pentecostal church shaped my life and spiritual journey from an early age. In my church, I experienced worship that was vibrant, preaching that was passionate, testimonies that were stirring, and the altar was active.

People would go to the altar for many reasons. Some would come in before service and cry out to God for His presence and purposes to be accomplished in the coming services. Others would flock to the altar during worship services physically pressing into God's presence, many were invited to come and be prayed for, and all were encouraged to come to the altar following the message for their own personal encounter with God. The altar represented the most sacred space to connecting with God for spiritual transformation.

My friend Rick DuBose has written a masterpiece on building a life and ministry of prayer. He reminds us that prayer is something the enemy does not want us to participate in, because whoever controls the altar controls the outcome.

People today are desperate for a sacred space to connect with God.

*In Jesus' Name* is not a book on the theology of prayer— yet it is loaded with a lot of theological truths—instead, it is an inspirational piece to help you catch a glimpse of the power of your effective, fervent praying. As you begin to understand the personal altar, the home altar, the core altar, the miracle altar, and the salvation altar, I'm confident prayer will become more than good intention but a regular habit.

My prayer is that you won't just read this book on prayer, but you will step into an activity of prayer and discover how prayer will help you reach your potential in Christ.

—Doug Clay, general superintendent of
the Assemblies of God

# INTRODUCTION

If we really understood the effect that prayer has on the world and our lives, the Church would become a place of continual prayer. We would pray without ceasing. Believers would start their days with effectual prayer, and every Christian family would have a well-worn family altar. If we really understood the power of prayer, it would change the way we pray.

I hope that reading this book will spur you on to greater prayer. I hope these few pages shine a light on how prayer works and how much prayer affects the outcome of our lives and ministries. I hope you learn how to effectively participate in it.

I wrote this book not because wonderful books on prayer don't already exist—they do, and many have helped me in my journey of prayer. But this book is different. I have discovered a viewpoint for prayer that I have not found written in any of the classic works on prayer. I strongly believe that what you are about to read comes from Scripture, and it has been personally useful in keeping me motivated and engaged in effectual prayer. My hope is that this book will do the same for you.

I have prayed not only that I would do the subject justice but that the Holy Spirit would use these written words to help you become wonderfully powerful in prayer. I pray that God would make you one of the greatest threats to the devil the world has ever seen! Remember, whoever controls the altar controls the outcome.

# ONE

# The Throne Room Above

*For the eyes of the Lord range throughout the earth to strengthen those whose hearts are fully committed to him.*

*2 Chronicles 16:9*

The sanctuary wasn't very full for the 6 a.m. open prayer time. The lights were low, and the event organizers played quiet background music, setting the atmosphere for prayer. We planned to pray for an hour or so, grab breakfast together, and be back for the opening morning sessions. Our church staff had traveled together from Texas to Missouri to participate in our fellowship's Call to Prayer conference. Prayer had long been a focus of our church and my own life. I saw the event as a good opportunity for both me and our staff to continue growing in prayer. That morning, I did what I do most mornings: I quieted my heart and reminded myself of the command to approach the throne of grace with boldness (see Hebrews 4:16). I dropped to my knees at a pew near the back of the sanctuary.

Morning prayer had long been my routine, whether at home, in my study, or traveling; however, my experience of prayer that morning was anything but typical. As quickly as my knees hit the floor, I was caught up into something far bigger than I had anticipated. The way I prayed would never be the same. I was about to experience the most transformative moment of prayer I had ever had.

My original career plans were for business. I grew up in a pastor's home, but I wasn't prepared or interested in serving as a pastor myself. As hard as I worked, God's blessing never seemed to be on my list of business goals. Nothing I did quite worked. So, with some reluctance, I finally submitted to God's calling and took a job as a youth pastor. I quickly realized I didn't have a clue what I was doing. I didn't know how to be a pastor. I didn't know how to lead anyone. And I didn't know where to turn for help.

I found a small room at the far end of the church I served that was tucked back behind the choir room, and I began to pray. It was a moment of absolute honesty before the Lord. I admitted to God I didn't know what I was doing. I didn't know what to do next. I didn't want this just to be a profession. I had been around too many pastors who seemed to be faking it. I wanted to do it with power—power that I didn't have and didn't know how to get. I was twenty-four years old, and I prayed that if God had really called me to be a pastor, would He help me do it.

That day, tucked away in a back room of a country church, God didn't pour out the power of His Spirit in any remarkable way, but He did give me a hunger. He gave me a hunger to grow and find a way forward through prayer. That prayer of youthful desperation became a habit of daily prayer, a habit of seeking a new word from God each day, and a habit of recognizing my daily need for His power.

Things did begin to change. Youth began responding. Miracles started happening. God's hand was more and more evident. It wasn't hard for me to connect those dots. When I prayed, God moved. When I attempted the work in my own power, it failed. Even at a young age, I developed a deep conviction that real ministry is about prayer.

> Prayer is not a static practice. Prayer is something we learn to do and something we continue to grow into.

As God moved me into various positions and seasons of ministry, the one constant was my commitment to pray. All I really knew how to do was pray. I watched as God answered those prayers in remarkable ways. We witnessed so many miracles during one season that a local newspaper journalist visited our church and published our story. We witnessed new revivals and watched the church grow. I preached the Gospel and witnessed the miraculous. Prayer was the only explanation for any of it. I knew from the beginning it was not me.

It is important to remember that prayer is not a static practice. We grow in prayer. I understood it more with each passing day, and I increasingly recognized my dependence on it for accomplishing anything meaningful. Prayer is something we learn to do and something we continue to grow into. To this day, I still want to understand prayer more.

I can take you back to the very place I bowed to pray that morning at 6 a.m. As my knees hit the floor and my eyes closed, I found myself suddenly someplace else. I knew I was still kneeling at that pew, but by the Spirit, I was taken into a higher place. I knew immediately, instinctively, where I was. I was experiencing the throne room of heaven.

I had never experienced anything like it before. It wasn't so much a vision as it was a moment of realization, an insight into so many of the images and descriptions I had encountered throughout Scripture. Suddenly, by God's grace and the power of the Holy Spirit, the pieces of those passages locked into place before my eyes. In that moment, what men like John, Isaiah, and Ezekiel had long described was mine as well. I was given an experience of the throne room above.

I have nothing to add to Scripture. What I experienced that morning was not a new revelation or some secret prayer with which I was entrusted. Far from it. What I experienced was a deeper understanding of what we all have, what Scripture has long offered each of us. But the things of Scripture are so easily neglected. We often fail to take advantage of the fullness they offer us.

It was immediately clear to me that I was not there for spectacle or simply to be impressed. I was given this insight to change the way I prayed. I was given this experience so that I might realize the real power of prayer and what takes place when we approach His throne room with boldness. I was being stretched and formed into a deeper way of praying. I was being taught to appreciate and to improve upon what I had long been doing.

I want to offer you what I saw and how it has transformed the way I pray. My hope is that these descriptions will move us to search Scripture again. I hope it will move us to recognize the grace we have been given, this remarkable gift of access to the throne room of God. May we never again pray casually or with indifference. May God give all of us a special insight into His heart and to the unique attention He gives to the words of our prayers.

> We do not enter His throne room symbolically— when we bow our heads to pray, we are there.

May we realize that we do not enter His throne room symbolically—when we bow our heads to pray, we are there.

## The Throne

The first thing that drew my eye was His throne. It was to my left. With my peripheral vision, I could only see its base, but I knew what it was. I knew who it was. There was an overwhelming sense of His presence and a sense of its immense significance to everything around it. It is still the most difficult part for me to describe. I am sure, however,

17

that you have also sensed the presence of God in ways that are difficult to articulate.

I knew I was in the presence of God. I knew I was before His throne, and I knew I was in His throne room. He was seated in power over everything else I experienced. I couldn't bring myself to look at Him. I knew I wasn't supposed to. To simply be before Him in His presence was enough. I was there by His grace.

My sense was like that so often described in Scripture and experienced in prayer: His presence humbled me. We realize His holiness and our true position of humble reverence. There was no sense of fear, not the kind that would cause you to run. There was, instead, a sense of awe that leaves you quiet and still. It was right that He was being worshiped; He was rightfully seated at the center of all things.

I also recognized that there was a place beside God on His great throne, but no one was seated in it. I knew who it belonged to—Jesus Christ. He shared completely in the power, authority, and holiness of God. It would soon be clear to me why His seat was empty.

**The Circle of Thrones**

As I began to look around, I realized that I was encircled by even more thrones—twenty-four of them. The first was placed to the left of God's throne, and the rest formed an enormous circle that eventually connected back to God's right. I remembered John's description of these thrones in the book of Revelation (see Revelation 4:2–4). These were the seats of the twenty-four elders: twelve for the apostles, and twelve for the tribes of Israel.

Above these thrones, the four cherubim were flying and singing their praise, "Holy, holy, holy" (verse 8). It was echoed by those who sat on the circle of thrones.

In Isaiah's vision of the throne room, it struck me that he didn't mention these thrones. They are central to John's vision in the New Testament. Perhaps in Isaiah's day, these thrones had yet to be fully seated. The throne room was being shaped by the work of Jesus and His apostles. What happened on earth was being reflected in the expanding worship of the throne room itself.

It was also obvious to me that the layout of these thrones was significant. They were intentionally arranged in the shape of a circle. This circle is often alluded to in Scripture as the "circle of the earth" (Isaiah 40:22). Those words suddenly took on new significance.

## The Earth and the Sea of Glass

One of the details I remember most clearly is what Scripture calls the sea of glass (see Revelation 4:6; 15:2). Within the ring of thrones was a massive surface that appeared like clear crystal. As I looked closer, however, beneath the glass was the earth stretched in such a way as to be entirely visible at once.

We know that the earth is round. It rotates on an axis giving us light and shadow, and it circles the sun in a sweeping annual orbit. In this heavenly reality, though, all of it was visible and present at once. The whole earth was laid out

19

before the throne of God, encircled by the thrones of the elders. All of heaven peered down through this glass floor, the earth always before them.

This was not a physical description but a witness to the ever-present attention of God. The whole earth is always before Him. When He looks down from His throne, He simultaneously sees every island, every nation, every city, every person. It is all before Him. His feet rested on this sea of glass, this image of all creation.

Immediately, I remembered the words spoken to Isaiah, "Heaven is my throne, and the earth is my footstool" (Isaiah 66:1). I finally understood it. All creation was there, always before Him, unfolded across the floor of His throne. He ruled over it all.

## The Intercessions of Jesus

Across this glassy image of the earth, Jesus was walking. He walked across this sea of glass as He had walked across the waters of Galilee. As Jesus walked, the image of the earth beneath Him began to move. With each step He took, the world shifted. Cities and nations began to burst into light. Perhaps it was what John described when he saw Jesus walking amongst the candlesticks (see Revelation 2:1). I had the distinct impression that Jesus was still doing the same, walking now amongst the churches spread over all the globe, each church burning brightly on the earth.

There was a striking interactivity between Jesus and the earth below Him. Not only did the earth shift beneath His feet, but it zoomed in, focusing on cities, streets, and individual homes. The movements weren't random; something was happening, some purpose with each shift.

I then heard Jesus praying. As He walked and as the earth moved, He was interceding. With each place He stood, Jesus turned to face the throne of God and prayed for those whose lives were beneath Him. Again, those prayers were not random. The lights glowing and building across the map seemed to intensify as Jesus took up their prayers. The prayers of earth were rising up to Jesus, and He was amplifying them before God. The interactivity was not just geographical; it was spiritual. Jesus was connected to these places on earth by His intercessory prayer. The prayers of earth were taking on new momentum as they were prayed in Jesus' name.

How many times had I prayed "in Jesus' name" and not fully realized in what I was participating? It had long been the way I had concluded my prayers; however, now I understand the real power of what I had been saying. It is not just a formality, a concluding phrase similar to signing a letter with "sincerely." When we pray in the name of Jesus, we are offering our prayers up into the throne room to the One who intensifies them in the unique privilege of His relationship with God. When we pray in Jesus' name, our prayers are magnified and released with a greater authority.

John was right when he described Jesus' voice as the sound of many waters. Jesus' prayers are not like ours, limited to these single tongues and thoughts. His prayers are filled with the prayers of believers all over the world. The prayers upon

21

His lips were like rivers, rivers of prayers streaming from the earth, through Him, and into the throne room of God.

Your prayers are not in some heavenly queue, some line they wait in to come before God. No, Jesus prays them all as they rise to Him. Never have I spoken a prayer in Jesus' name the same way again.

## The Balcony of Saints

As I watched these prayers rise from the earth, filling the throne room by Jesus' voice, I began to notice the scale of the room. I had been focused on what was below me, but now I began to see the immensity of the space above. Circling the throne room was a great balcony, a mezzanine filled with saints peering down and watching all this movement and action below. From their vantage point, they could witness how the activity of heaven was directly connected with the activity on earth. They saw through the throne room and down into creation.

> Their prayers existed in the throne room even after they had passed on earth.

They were witnesses to the prayers of earth and the divine responsiveness. I began to understand the power of their witness in ways I hadn't before. They were not only witnesses to the work God had done in their own lives, but by their position in the heavens, they were witnesses to the work of God across all time and creation.

I watched as saints were individually called forward by name to the front of the balcony. They were being invited to witness something unique to them. I realized that these saints had died with prayers that had not been fulfilled in their lifetime. But those prayers remained in heaven. Their prayers existed in the throne room even after they had passed on earth. Now, these men and women were being welcomed to watch as those prayers they had long prayed were answered on earth below. They were being called forward to see their prayers answered, the fulfillment of hours spent petitioning heaven. No prayer had been ignored. No prayer had been lost. No prayer had been forgotten. Their prayers waited in the throne room until their sovereign moment, and they, by God's calling, were now able to watch them being fulfilled below.

Grandparents were witnessing the grandchildren they prayed for until they died finally receive salvation. They were witnessing the marriages of their children finally restored. Saints were witnessing fresh revivals poured out on the churches they had long served and for which they had long prayed. Nations were being transformed before the eyes of those who had given their lives for those places. Having not seen the fruit of their prayers while alive, they now witnessed it from this heavenly vantage point.

Not only were they witnessing it, but by being called forward, all of heaven was acknowledging their participation in these great movements of God. As they witnessed it, they worshiped. They declared the goodness and faithfulness of God.

More of these saints were being called forward from the earth itself, ascending from earth and through the sea of glass to take their place amongst the saints. It was as Stephen had seen it at his martyrdom. The book of Acts records, "But Stephen, full of the Holy Spirit, looked up to heaven and saw the glory of God, and Jesus standing at the right hand of God" (7:55).

From his vantage point on earth, Stephen saw up through the sea of glass and into the throne room above. Soon he would be brought up into it himself. How Stephen must have rejoiced as he took his own place among those saints and witnessed the answer to his own prayers, the spread of the Gospel across Jerusalem, Judea, Samaria, and the ends of the earth.

## The Arena of Angels

As this balcony of saints grew in worship, it was echoed still louder by an ascending arena of the angels above. A great stadium of heavenly hosts—row after row rising above the throne room—surrounded the room. John counted them as ten thousand times ten thousand (see Revelation 5:11). They were too numerous to count. These angels were falling on their faces and echoing the words of the passing cherubim, "Holy, holy, holy!"

Suddenly the whole stadium and the throne room below were filled with the sounds of worship, glorifying God. And as Jesus prayed, specific angels were being commissioned from that arena down into the earth. At times it was a single angel, while at other times it was armies of them, thousands of angels descending into the earth.

I couldn't see where they were going or the work they were doing. As they descended, they disappeared into the details below. But I understood that they were commissioned specifically by God into those places. Prayer had necessitated their arrival, and God had ordered their direction.

All of these images combined into a clear sense of the enormous movement and energy of heaven. I stood gazing at the spectacular energy of the heavens and the earth below. It was alive with the activity of prayer: intercession, worship, declarations, heartfelt petitions, and the movement of saints and angels. Heaven was constantly in motion, responding and moving in coordination with the prayers of earth. There were no missing pieces, no thrones still empty. Everything was active and responsive to prayer. Everything was coordinated—never chaotic—but orchestrated in constant motion. All of it was a culmination of prayer.

By the power of the name of Jesus, we had access to it all. Our prayers rose into this throne room and moved it, stirred it. Heaven and earth moved by the prayers we prayed in Jesus' name.

### The Question

And just as quickly as it came, it was over. I found myself still kneeling at that same pew in the back of a mostly empty sanctuary. I wasn't quite sure what to do. Then, I sensed as clearly as I had the vision of the throne room a question from the Holy Spirit: *What did you learn?*

This had not been for my own amusement or some spiritual affirmation or encouragement. The Spirit wanted me to learn something about all the prayers I had been praying for so long.

I also knew by the power of the Spirit what I was meant to have learned. I live in the throne room. It is not some separate place. It is not up there, somewhere off in the distance. It isn't some abstract theological concept. The whole earth is there in the middle of it. All our days are there before Him. There is nothing He does not see. We live and pray in the midst of His throne room.

Heaven and earth are one. I finally understood why God said He would one day destroy the heavens and the earth, and why He would form new ones. He cannot destroy one without the other, no more than we can live in one and not the other. The heavens are His throne, and the earth is His footstool. They are joined by prayer.

You are there right now. You are in His throne room. When we pray, we take our proper place in that throne room. When we pray, we acknowledge that we are in it. We have access to everything in heaven. By your prayers, you move heaven. By your prayers, Jesus moves and prays, angels descend, saints bear witness, and God acts.

We cannot forget why God calls us to approach His throne room boldly. By grace, He has given us access to all of it. God's heart is that you would realize what you have. You have a place in that throne room. You have it now. By prayer, you are already a participant in the heavens above. In the name of Jesus, your prayer is spoken by the Savior Himself.

We have made too little of prayer. Sure, we have made it a discipline, a personal practice, a matter of habit, but we have not fully realized how much prayer changes things. So much depends on prayer. So much has been given to us through prayer.

God is probably not asking you for something new. You probably already pray. But He is asking you to recognize and take advantage of everything He has already given you through prayer. Prayer is our way forward into all things.

For a long time, I kept this experience to myself. I knew I needed to grow into it. I needed to work this reality into my own life. Finally, a time came when I attempted to humbly share it with my congregation. I watched as it changed my church in the same ways it had changed me. I watched as people began to pray in new ways, and as they, too, moved their lives into the reality of His throne room.

That was years ago. I had always understood that moment before His throne as a gift to the church I led and to me. But a couple of years ago, I felt the Spirit again prompt me. God is about to do something new in the world. Prayer is the key, the beginning, the way forward. It is time we take full advantage of what we have by prayer.

I want to humbly offer you what I have received. I want to be a part of whatever God is preparing to do. I want to participate fully in everything happening in the throne room above. I want you and your church in on it, too.

27

# TWO

# Our Prayers Below

*Daniel . . . went home to his upstairs room where the windows opened toward Jerusalem. Three times a day he got down on his knees and prayed, giving thanks to his God, just as he had done before.*

*Daniel 6:10*

The heavens above are in constant motion. God is moving, Jesus is interceding, and the saints are worshiping and bearing witness to prayers being constantly answered. As the psalmist put it, "The heavens declare the glory of God" (Psalm 19:1). They are alive with His glory. Experiencing this energized activity of heaven changed the way I understood how our prayers are heard. The throne room is filled with our prayers, moved by our prayers. But on earth, it is easy to feel less inspired. The heavens may be alive, but often our times of prayer feel stagnant and cold. When we are alone in a moment of prayer, it can feel as if nothing is happening.

As a pastor, I have counseled countless people who feel their prayers don't make a difference. People feel as if their prayers go unheard. They feel as though their prayers are prayed into an empty void. We may feel an obligation or a desire to pray, but we aren't sure what really happens when we do. Where do our prayers go? It is easy to lose the connection between the throne room above and our praying below. We pray, but we aren't sure what is happening or what impact our prayers have.

> The heavens may be alive, but often our times of prayer feel stagnant and cold.

But God is not ignoring our prayers. He is not distracted. In fact, prayer isn't something we are left to figure out on our own. We do not pray into an empty sky; we pray into an active throne room. We pray into a throne room moved by our prayers.

Scripture offers us the powerful prayers of men and women from whom we can learn. By them, we better understand why we pray, how we should pray, and what happens when we do. Daniel is one of the most powerful men of prayer of all time. Daniel's prayer life can teach us a lot about the importance of prayer and what really happens when we pray.

## Daniel and the Dangers of Prayer

Mention Daniel and most people remember a den full of lions. It is that old Sunday School story we grew up with.

Certainly, it is a story about how God protects His people, just as He did Shadrach, Meshach, and Abednego, who were three of Daniel's friends. God is faithful to rescue us in our moments of need, whether that be from flames or lions. But Daniel's story is about far more than escaping the jaws of beasts. Daniel's story is about the power of prayer and how our prayers on earth move heaven above.

Daniel was a young Jewish exile living in the great city of Babylon. Having laid siege to Jerusalem, the Babylonians carried off the best and the brightest of Israel, assimilating their skills and talents into Babylonian society. Daniel had been selected to serve in the king's palace. He was already recognized for his talent and potential. It was a position of favor, but it came with unique temptations and challenges. Daniel was offered food and alcohol that violated his lifestyle as a Jew. Refusing to eat that food risked his position and possibly his life. Still, Daniel refused. He continued to observe his Jewish practices and worship Israel's God alone. Daniel refused to live as the world around him did, even when it cost him. He may have lost his home, but he would not lose his God. Though he served in Babylon, he continued to serve the God of Israel.

God blessed Daniel's faithfulness with wisdom beyond that of any other advisor in Babylon. That wisdom allowed him to rise quickly in influence and to gain favor in the culture around him. Externally, things seemed good for Daniel. But Daniel was engaged in something that threatened the demonic powers of that pagan nation. Daniel not only continued his Jewish lifestyle, but he also continued to pray.

Daniel prayed that God would restore his people and their nation.

Nothing threatens the work of the enemy more than prayer. You can gain political power, you can accumulate wealth, you can even use your platform to share your faith, but nothing threatens the work of Satan more than when we pray. Daniel had to be stopped. It was his prayers that the devil was concerned about. It was his praying that put all he thought he had accomplished at risk.

For a long time, Daniel had made it his routine to pray at the altar of his window. That window faced toward Jerusalem. So daily, Daniel would kneel in his window and pray for his home, his people, and the future of Jerusalem. People saw Daniel praying. They understood by his devotion and routine how important it was to him. Daniel had an altar. That altar was more important to his life and work than any governmental position or Babylonian favor.

**Nothing threatens the work of the enemy more than prayer.**

Though Daniel served with integrity, and maybe because of it, he had enemies. Motivated by demonic inspiration, pride, and insecurity, Daniel's enemies plotted to silence him. They confronted Daniel where they knew he had the most effect: they would attempt to silence his prayers.

They knew they could not tempt Daniel, so they formed a plan to trick the king into silencing Daniel's prayers. They convinced the king to issue a decree that for thirty days no one could pray to any god except to the king himself. This decree made Daniel's daily prayers an act of treason and

32

punishable by death. They knew Daniel's faithfulness. The decree would silence him either by fear or by death.

Notice how Daniel's enemies didn't try to trap him in sin or tempt him into compromise. They struck at Daniel's strength, the thing that most threatened them. They tried to keep him from praying.

What did Daniel do? He did what he always did. He went to his altar in the window and prayed. No law or scheme could keep him from it. Not even threats against his life. Nothing was more important to Daniel than prayer.

Why is Satan so opposed to prayer? Why was it Daniel's prayers that stirred his enemies to action? We may feel as if our prayers go unheard, or we may feel as though our prayers are not answered, but Satan does not share that opinion. Satan wants to keep us from praying because he knows how much prayer matters. He knows the power of prayer perhaps even more than we do.

Scripture repeatedly reminds us that there are things happening around us that our senses cannot recognize. We live in a world of spiritual conflict. Paul explained to the Ephesians, "Our struggle is not against flesh and blood, but against . . . the spiritual forces of evil in the heavenly realms" (Ephesians 6:12). Satan fears prayer because prayer moves the unseen. Satan understands that he is most vulnerable when we pray, when we take up this struggle against the powers of darkness through prayer. It is no surprise that he will use every tactic at his disposal to keep us from praying. From simple distractions to legal limitations, Satan seeks to silence your prayers, too.

It was true in Daniel's day and true in ours. It is no coincidence that prayer continues to be under attack. It always has been and always will be, as long as the enemy is about his work. Private, personal prayer may be permitted (though it is often ridiculed and increasingly neglected) but public prayer is fiercely attacked. The Barna Group has reported that of the Americans who pray, only two percent pray audibly with another person or group, and only two percent participate in praying with their church.[1]

Perhaps Daniel could have prayed privately and no one would have known. He could have stepped away from his window and prayed somewhere out of sight. He could have avoided the whole conflict by keeping his prayers to himself. Certainly, Daniel did also pray in private, but what got Daniel in trouble was his refusal to give up public prayer. He would not hide what he was doing.

When prayer gets reduced to only a private and personal matter, we limit it, and we limit the ability of believers to learn how to do it. People are left to figure it out on their own. Our congregants grow frustrated and feel unprepared. They may talk about prayer, but it becomes increasingly less important in their lives. We, too, assimilate to the world around us and gradually lose our knowledge and passion for prayer. It takes believers like Daniel to keep it alive in a place like Babylon.

When Jesus taught His disciples to pray, He did it by praying with them. They prayed together. When they faced challenges, they gathered to pray. When they sought the Spirit, they gathered in an upper room. When one of them was in danger, they gathered in a home and prayed. The New Testament is filled with people praying together and praying in public.

God's people pray. It is what we do; therefore, praying must be at the center of who your church is and what it does. Everything is shaped by prayer. Every church must build a ministry of prayer. It can't be just a small group that meets once a week. It can't be just a few passionate people, though that is a great place to start. Prayer must energize every part of your church. You must teach people how to pray. You must practice praying with them. You must make space for it in your services and calendars. You must commit to praying privately and publicly. It is prayer that moves the heavens and prayer that energizes the church. It is prayer that ushers in revival and pushes back the darkness. It is prayer that threatens the enemy and releases God's power.

> Daniel believed that using his authority in the spirit world was more important than using his influence in the political world.

Don't get distracted. As a church leader, there is nothing more important in your life and church than prayer. And there is nothing you will be more tempted to neglect.

Daniel's actions proved that he believed more in the effectiveness of prayer than all his other gifts and talents. Daniel had wisdom and influence. He knew how to lead and administrate. He held a powerful position and had access to critical resources. Daniel knew how to be a great leader. But when he faced challenges, when he really needed things done, he went to his window, knelt at his altar, and prayed. Before he was anything else, Daniel was a man of prayer.

Daniel believed that using his authority in the spirit world was more important than using his influence in the political world. That is a lesson for us as leaders. When we work and lead without praying, are we not making the statement that our actions and skills are more powerful and more important than our prayers? When our churches see the emphasis we put on planning, resources, and strategy, do we not risk them seeming more important to us than prayer? Too often they are.

The demonic forces at work around Daniel confronted him at the center of his power—they confronted his praying. The devil would love to completely stop the church and all its good works, but if he can only stop one aspect, it will always be prayer. Satan fears it more than a church service with great music or a dynamic sermon. He is content to let the church fill its time with anything that will keep it from the altar. And too often, it is the altar that is most neglected.

No one could question Daniel's priorities. No one could question his source of power or be confused about what mattered most to him. Daniel's life and leadership were marked by prayer. He was willing to die for it. What marks yours?

## Evaluating Prayer

Building a ministry of prayer begins with some important self-evaluations. It is going to take honesty. It is easy to evaluate your life based on what you achieve. We are good at evaluating our own successes, influence, and accomplishments. But the enemy is happy to let us accumulate good things if it keeps us from what is most important.

Evaluating your prayer life isn't just about how much time you spend praying or how frequently you pray. Certainly, time and frequency matter, but they are the natural fruit of a deeper belief and commitment to prayer, a life lived in His throne room.

So, ask yourself, What are the things that keep you from praying? For some, it is time. With busy schedules and constant demands, prayer gets pressed out of the day. After all, God isn't knocking at your office door, texting you problems, or calling with requests. It is easy for external demands to fill up your time and end up with your prayers getting diminished.

> What are the things that keep you from praying?

For some, prayer is limited by the prioritization of other relationships. Part of being a pastor is loving and spending time with people. It is possible to prioritize relationships with others over your relationship with God. In fact, the constant need to be around others can be a way of avoiding yourself and God. Is it possible for relationships to keep you from prayer?

I heard a story about one of our great prayer warriors that went something like this. They said he had a close friend who had been away for a long time who came unannounced into his study expecting to be welcomed with excitement. Instead, he was greeted with hesitance and was requested to come back later. It was the prayer warrior's time of prayer and communion with God, and he would not allow anything or anyone to violate it. Even though he loved and looked forward to his time with the old friend, his time with God was of greater value.

For some, family is a constant distraction. For others, they are distracted by the open-door policy to the church that fills the time that should belong to God. Establishing times and closing the door to the outside is even more required to those of us who love being with people more than any other part of our life. We need to join the old prayer warrior I just spoke about and make our prayer time as holy as a Sunday morning service.

> To step into the throne room of God is to lay down our attempts at control.

Or perhaps it's interests and hobbies. After hard days of work and the stress that comes with it, we look for opportunities to relax and pursue the things we enjoy. There is certainly nothing wrong with hobbies, but they can replace important things. They can distract us from higher priorities. To truly grow in prayer will always mean giving up something to be with God.

But maybe the most difficult evaluation to make is to look at our need for control. Trying to stay in control of our life often keeps us from prayer. When I experienced the reality of God's throne room, one of the most important truths that I learned is that my life is lived in His presence. That means my life is not lived in my own throne room—it is lived in His. To recognize that I am before His throne is to recognize He is rightfully in control.

To step into the throne room of God is to lay down our attempts at control. Remember how the elders laid down their crowns before His throne? Each time we pray, we do something similar. We lay down our control. We lay down our authority. We lay down our plans and projects. We seek His will. That can be an uncomfortable consequence if we are desperate to stay in control. Many do not pray because they know giving up control risks too much. We attempt to plan and lead out of our own power.

## On Earth As It Is in Heaven

There must have been something about how Jesus prayed that stood out to His disciples. The disciples grew up in a world of prayer. Prayer was not a new concept for them. They had heard prayers at the synagogue, at religious festivals in Jerusalem, and probably from the mouths of their parents as they grew. The disciples had certainly prayed themselves. But as they watched and listened to Jesus pray, they sensed something different. Their request was as simple as a child. "Jesus, will you teach us to pray?" (Luke 11:1). They wanted to pray like Jesus.

What Jesus offered them is remembered as the Lord's Prayer. Much of it is simple to understand. He encouraged them to pray for daily bread, to pray for forgiveness, and to pray for protection from temptation and evil. But there is a line that has always intrigued me. Jesus taught them to pray that God's will would be done on earth as it is in heaven. Right there in the middle of Jesus' prayer, He acknowledges the unique connectedness of life here below and the reality of heaven above. Our prayers connect us to heaven. Our prayers connect us to the throne room and to the power of God.

I have prayed that prayer countless times and have come to believe that it requires a humility to recognize that we cannot change the world through our earthly power. It offers us an opportunity to stir heaven into action. We move heaven to see things changed on earth.

There are things that no matter how hard you try you cannot fix. There are things on earth that no earthly power can change. To give all your time and energy to mere earthly projects is to be significantly stunted in what is possible. We pray partly because we realize how limited we are in our earthly possessions and power. We pray because we need things we can't do on our own. Jesus recognized both the limitations of earth and our need for God's will from heaven.

When Jesus described how the reality of heaven has an impact on earth, He was helping us realize that heaven must be affected before the earth can be changed. Every earthly struggle is preceded by a heavenly one. Our earthly power may be limited, but when heaven is stirred, there is nothing on earth that cannot be changed. To pray for God's will on earth as it is in heaven is to pray that heaven might be moved to accomplish things on earth that we otherwise could not.

I believe Daniel understood that remarkable truth about prayer. What made Daniel so powerful and so threatening to the leaders of his day was not his personal skills or talent, as great as they were. What made Daniel a threat was the way he prayed. Daniel understood how to move heaven. His prayers released angels and instigated heavenly war. Once he had moved heaven, there was nothing his prayers could not accomplish on earth. Daniel could change earthly kingdoms by the power of his prayers in heaven. That is what the earthly rulers feared.

Daniel had been praying for years that Israel's exile would come to an end. In response, God gave Daniel a series of visions. He gave Daniel a glimpse into things to come and things that were already underway in heaven. Daniel saw a vision of a series of kings and kingdoms. These were kingdoms of earth, rulers who used earthly power to rule. They were powerful and ruthless and set themselves up in opposition to God. But they were not the only reality.

Though they seemed unbeatable and Israel's future seemed hopeless, an angel explained to Daniel, "Do not be afraid, Daniel. Since the first day that you set your mind to gain understanding and to humble yourself before your God, your words were heard, and I have come in response to them" (Daniel 10:12).

Though these earthly kings imagined themselves supreme, Daniel's words were being heard in heaven. The angel went on to explain that he and others had been commissioned from heaven to confront these earthly powers. There was already a heavenly war underway because of Daniel's prayers.

This was the reason Satan, and those earthly rulers he maneuvered, were determined to end Daniel's prayers. And it is for this reason that Daniel was determined not to stop. He didn't pray publicly to make a point. He didn't pray just to resist the culture around him. Daniel prayed because he

41

knew that as heaven was moved, what he was praying for would be done on earth. He prayed because it mattered most. He prayed to change things. No hobby, work, or relationship could keep him from it. Prayer defined Daniel's life. He knew it was where he was most powerful.

If you try to bend a tree, you can't do it. Lean on it, push on it, take heavy machinery to it and you still can't bend it. Years of unnoticed growth have fixed it. But it is easy to bend a fresh shoot, a growing sapling. You can do it with your fingers. If you hold it, it will grow bent. You can make it any shape if you show up every day and apply even small pressure. In the end, no one will be able to straighten it out.

We can change the world. But it will not happen by the world's power. It will not be changed by momentary bursts of strength. We must show up every day and move heaven. As heaven is stirred, so it will be done on earth. It doesn't require great wealth. It doesn't require political power. It doesn't require special skills or knowledge. It requires people, like Daniel, who are willing to humble themselves and go daily into the throne room above. It requires people being willing to fight a spiritual battle. It requires people willing to pray. If we are willing, there is nothing on earth that cannot be moved. Our prayers connect earth and heaven.

## My Hope for You and Your Church

I hope you become like Daniel. The world needs you to be. But really, my hope is that your church would raise up a generation of Daniels. The Church must recapture its focus on prayer. Our power in this world depends on it. This book exists to help you do it. You need a deeper prayer life, and you need to lead and cultivate places of prayer across your congregation.

I want you to consider how much time you have given to cultivating leadership skills or defining your church's strategy. Those are important and necessary tasks, but they are not the tools Daniel used to overcome Satan or oppose Babylon. They are not the focus of Jesus' lesson on prayer. You will do more by prayer than you will by leadership development or church strategy. The altar is the place of change. The altar is the way forward. Whoever controls the altar controls the outcome.

> Whoever controls the altar controls the outcome.

It is my deepest belief that if we could all truly understand how powerful and effective prayer is, the Church would be transformed into a place filled with constant prayer, believers would find their days dependent on prayer, and families would center their life together around it.

Just as Daniel defined his life by that altar in the window, I want to help you do it—first in your own life and then in the congregation you lead or attend. I want to help you build the five critical altars that will help you and your congregation discover and experience the power of prayer.

43

# THREE

## An Altar In Between

*Then Noah built an altar to the Lord and, taking some of all the clean animals and clean birds, he sacrificed burnt offerings on it.*

*Genesis 8:20*

Having finally stepped out of the ark, Noah's first impulse was to build an altar. Because of God's warning, he and his family had been spared the floodwaters that had covered the earth. They had drifted in their ark for days, suspended between heaven and earth. If not for God's kindness and Noah's faith, they would have perished, too. The ark had come to rest on land again, and Noah stepped out into a new world. Before he did anything else, he worshiped. He built an altar and made a sacrifice. It is the first altar recorded in Scripture, but it certainly is not the last.

45

Altars have long been a place created to connect heaven and earth. Through sacrifice, they allow us to bring the things of this world and offer them to God. The smoke of Noah's burnt offering was a pleasant aroma to God as it drifted upward toward heaven. These altars became a common way for God's people to connect the needs of their life—their prayers and worship—with the throne room of God.

Elijah constructed an altar before he prayed to heaven and called down fire as a sign to the pagan prophets and the onlooking crowd of Israelites. Ezra made the reconstruction of Jerusalem's altar a priority in his work while rebuilding the city and the temple. Abraham built altars to mark places of God's promise. Even as Israel wandered through the wilderness, Moses kept finding places to draw away from the people to pray: mountains, tents, and altars.

> Altars have long been a place created to connect heaven and earth.

There wasn't a lot required to construct an altar. Some were simply stones piled upon one another. Some were carved, some crafted from bronze. Some were just earth, humble places where families gathered. Others were impressive and central to Israel's identity. The altar in the temple courtyard was seven and a half feet wide with a massive ramp that was used by priests to place daily sacrifices. Still, all these altars served the same basic purpose: they were a place to encounter God, a place to sacrifice, and a place to pray. They were a place where the things of earth rose to the throne room.

Jesus understood altars. Entering the temple and finding it overrun with merchants and money lenders, He cast them out, reminding them His Father's house would "be called a house of prayer" (Matthew 21:13). We no longer place sacrifices upon altars, but we still construct them, and Jesus understood that at the heart of every altar is a heart of prayer.

Altars are the intentional places we construct to remind us of the connection between heaven and earth. They are the places to which we return to pray. So, like our ancient brothers and sisters, we still build them. Perhaps not of the same design or materials, but we, too, find places to pray. We crawl to those places and offer our time, emotions, finances, and plans as a living sacrifice.

An altar doesn't need to be anything more than an open space at the back of your closet. But it does need to be somewhere. It does need to exist. And what matters most is what you do while you're there, while you're at that altar. What matters is your faithfulness to build them and the prayers your pray while at them.

An altar no longer needs to be built with stone or wood. It can be the steering wheel of a car, a chair in the den, or beside the bed in a hotel room. The altar is more about the prayer than the place or setting. It is anywhere and anytime that we decide to recognize our existence in the throne room of heaven. It is anytime we stop allowing ourselves to be limited to what we can see, when we bow our heads in faith and humility and say, "Our Father in heaven, we hallow Your name." I have made altars in hospital rooms, automobiles, airplane seats, kitchen tables, and most often my recliner in the basement. An altar is first and foremost a decision to recognize our need to submit to God and ask for His divine help.

## Developing a Culture of Prayer

While pastoring, I developed a tradition of praying for an hour each Saturday night. I would walk to the church, and then pace the empty sanctuary praying for the next day's service and the men and women who would be in attendance. The truth is, I also prayed for myself. I prayed that God would do in those services what I knew I was not capable of doing by my own talent or ability. I was desperate for God to move, and I wasn't sure what else to do but pray.

One Saturday night, I looked up, and a man from the congregation was standing at the back of the sanctuary watching me.

"What are you doing?" he asked.

"Praying," I responded.

He looked at me for a moment and asked, "Can I join you?"

It wasn't a program. It wasn't even really a prayer service. It wasn't a part of some strategy I had outlined for cultivating a movement of prayer in our church. But we were intentional. Every Saturday, we showed up with no other agenda than to pray. Eventually, a few others joined us. Word began to spread, and I made it official. Before long there were sometimes as many as one hundred of us praying together. It was an altar, a place where we met with God.

We often experienced powerful moves of the Spirit. While praying, someone would feel drawn to a particular seat. They would feel an urgency to pray over that place and the person who would sit there the next day, sensing that God had plans for that person. As Sunday came, we all witnessed hands risen for salvation from the very seats where they had sensed the Spirit's call to pray. We all sensed that our prayers were a part of something bigger than Saturday nights. Our passion for prayer and for the altar was growing.

Looking back, something in our congregation changed through those Saturday nights, something I was leading without realizing what it was. I now look back and recognize how those Saturday prayer meetings began to change the people in my church, and how they began to infuse our church with a new culture of prayer.

There is so much advice and there are so many techniques for how to change the culture of a church, but it isn't as complicated as it may sometimes seem. Culture is simply a set of shared values. Culture forms as a group of people begin to value similar things. Whatever we value most is what defines our culture. That is not hard to understand, but it can be extremely difficult to change.

Certainly, part of the challenge is getting people to value something new. But the real challenge of changing a church's culture is getting people to be honest about what they really do value. Most of us who have followed Jesus for any amount of time know the things we should value. But knowing something is valuable doesn't mean we actually value it. We may even all agree that something is valuable, but that does not mean that we, as a church, truly value it. We can know the value of a piece of art, a luxury car, or dinner at a five-star restaurant, but that doesn't mean we want it or are willing to pay for it. Knowing that it is valuable does not mean that we personally value it.

Prayer is like that. We know prayer is valuable. We know that it is a vital part of any believer's life, and we know that Jesus valued it. But we can know prayer is valuable without valuing it ourselves. I have never been in a church that didn't think prayer was valuable, but I have been in very few churches where prayer was a shared value.

That is all culture is. A culture of prayer simply means that your church both knows the value of prayer and personally values it themselves. To change the culture of your church, to create a new culture of prayer, you need only move prayer from a thing that is valuable to a thing your church actually values. It must be made one of the main things on the calendar and in the practice of leadership before it will become a high value in the culture of the church.

**What is the first thing you do when there is a need?**

I pose a simple question to test what your church currently values. What is the first thing you do when there is a need? Do you hold an emergency meeting? Do you start raising funds? Do you turn to your favorite online resource for advice? When the early Church found themselves facing a need, the first thing they did was pray. It is the pattern repeated again and again in the book of Acts. The early Church constantly gathered to pray. It was the first thing they did. It was the thing they valued most. It was their culture.

If you are going to call your church to prayer, if you are going to create a culture of prayer, if you are going to help the men and women in your church live in the throne room of God, it is going to take honesty about what you actually value as a community, and it is going to take intentionality to build new altars of prayer.

As our church began to grow in prayer, I became increasingly intentional about working prayer into every part of our time together and into our leadership development. We simplified our board's responsibilities and met for no other reason than prayer. The staff began to prioritize praying together each week, and we challenged one another to press deeper and expect more from our personal prayers. I didn't have the language for it at the time, but we were intentionally constructing altars. We were building places in which we could "approach God's throne of grace with confidence, so that we may receive mercy and find grace to help us in our time of need" (Hebrews 4:16). We were learning to approach God's throne of grace with confidence, because we needed mercy and grace to help us in our times of need.

We were crafting a new culture based on a valuable thing becoming the thing we valued most. It is possible for your church, too. I want to help you construct altars of your own, places where you can encounter God and connect heaven and earth, and places that will change the culture of your church.

## The Five Altars Every Church Needs

I want to introduce you to five altars of prayer every church must be intentional about building. They are not just a program or strategy. They are values, intentional practices that will help you move prayer forward in the priorities of your church. These altars will help you not only cultivate a new culture of prayer, but they will also help you encounter God and experience the power of His throne room.

In the coming chapters, I will unpack each of these altars to help you understand how to be intentional about each. I will offer you lessons from my life as well as give powerful examples from Scripture. But you will have to provide the intentionality. This book is not a theology of prayer. I didn't write this book so that you could learn about prayer. I wrote it so that it might inspire you to actually pray. I wrote it so that you might, by catching a glimpse of what you have in prayer, be moved to pray with a new focus. I wrote it to help you lead a change in your church's culture, to help you call your church to prayer.

### 1. The Personal Altar

If you want to lead a cultural change in your church, you must value your personal altar above all others. Everything you do and everything you are begins in prayer. It begins in the privacy of your own prayer altar. It begins in a willing sacrifice, in death, and in submitting your life to God. It is a secret place, a place where you discover who you are and where you grow in ever-increasing intimacy with your heavenly Father. If you are a pastor, your personal altar is the lid of your church's praying. If you are a parent, it is the lid of your family's altar. God has called you to value it and to lead from it. It starts here, your altar.

### 2. The Home Altar

We are called to make disciples. Disciples know how to pray, and they value it as a part of their life—not just on Sunday mornings. But the truth is many people simply don't know how to pray. They have seen it done, but no one has taught them how to do it themselves. The disciples requested that Jesus teach them to pray. Jesus took the time to do it. He showed them how to pray by His own prayers, and He taught them how to pray for themselves. We need families that value prayer, that pray together, that know how to pray, and that raise their kids to pray. A church that is serious about prayer will be serious about the home altar. They will be serious about teaching families to pray.

### 3. The Core Altar

Faith can be a spiritual gift. While all believers participate in it, God calls some men and women to extraordinary acts of faith and prayer. If God has given you a vision and has called you to lead His Church, He has also called men and women to join you in prayer. From that core of believers gathered in the Upper Room to the group that gathered daily in the temple to pray, there has always been a core committed to prayer. Cultivating a culture of prayer requires a core of people who are willing to lead the way. I want to help you identify that core, help you equip them to grow in prayer, and help you lead your church into a deeper culture of prayer.

### 4. The Miracle Altar

We all want to see miracles. Miracles demonstrate the power of God to the world. They show God's compassion, His power, and His credibility. But when we don't witness enough of the miraculous, it isn't because God is distant or unwilling. Too often, He finds people unprepared for His miraculous moves. God gave us clear instructions. He taught us how to pray with authority, how to lay hands on the sick, how to anoint with oil, and how to offer prayers with bold faith. God wants to do miracles in your church, but you need an altar, an intentional place, and a commitment to praying for the miraculous.

### 5. The Salvation Altar

Ultimately, there is a time when each person must come to the altar for themselves. Scripture is clear; a day is coming when every knee will bow and every tongue will confess that Jesus is Lord (see Philippians 2:10–11). By God's grace, we are each given an opportunity to recognize His authority and to humble our hearts and receive Him as our Savior. There is an altar of salvation that we must pray over and that we must invite every person to approach for themselves. The goal of every church is to welcome the lost into the Kingdom of God. So, we build altars where we call the world to repent, bow a knee, and receive Christ.

As we begin the work of building these five altars, I want to suggest that you take a moment to commit this process to prayer. When God moved on the hearts of His people, they often responded by building an altar as a reminder of what God had spoken to them. An altar can mark a new place of commitment.

It is easy for a moment of good intention to be lost. It is easy for a divine moment to be forgotten. But our call to prayer is too important to be neglected. Too much depends on it. Perhaps you need to take a moment to commemorate this moment. Stack up some stones if you must, but do not allow prayer to slip into the background of your life and ministry. We have work ahead, but it begins with intention. We will pray. We will lead churches that pray. We will enter heaven's throne room through our prayers. We will witness the miracles of God by prayer. We will control the outcomes by these altars of prayer.

# FOUR

# Building the Personal Altar

*But when you pray, go into your room, close the door and pray to your Father, who is unseen. Then your Father, who sees what is done in secret, will reward you.*

*Matthew 6:6*

Leading a church or family that prays begins with you. The first altar that must be built is your personal altar of prayer—your secret place with God. It doesn't matter where you lead, how big or small, a family or a church, God has given you a measure of authority. That authority is not just earthly power. As Jesus said, we are not like those earthly leaders who lord their power over people (see Matthew 20:25–26). The authority you have been given

57

is first and foremost a spiritual authority. It is formed by your time with God.

You have been given access to the throne room. You have been given the spiritual authority to lead and to come before the God of the universe. Your church and family will not be all that God intends them to be if you, as their leader, fail to step into the responsibility and authority God has given you. But spiritual authority doesn't begin on stage or with a microphone. It is not formed in a classroom or a board room. Spiritual authority is formed in a secret place of prayer.

> Spiritual authority is formed in a secret place of prayer.

Jesus made this point perfectly clear to His followers. Prayer did not begin with a public display. They weren't to pray as a display to the synagogue or on the street corners so that others could hear their prayers and be impressed. If you are looking for a reputation as someone who prays, that is the reward you will get. People may think you pray, but you won't have real spiritual authority, and you won't have the kind of divine relationship that moves heaven and earth.

Instead, Jesus commanded His followers, "When you pray, go into your room, close the door and pray to your Father, who is unseen. Then your Father, who sees what is done in secret, will reward you" (Matthew 6:6).

Jesus wasn't against praying in public. He prayed publicly over the bread and fish before the five thousand followers. He also prayed from the cross before the soldiers, and He often prayed with His disciples. But He understood that a life of prayer begins in private communion with God. If you want to pray, if you want to lead a church or a family that prays, start with a personal altar of prayer.

Jesus' disciples were impressed by His words and prayers not because they were spectacular or poetic. They were impressed because He prayed and spoke with authority and in intimacy with God. They sensed that He knew God and that He walked in a spiritual authority uncommon to other leaders and teachers. When they asked Jesus to teach them to pray as He did, Jesus didn't respond, "You could never do what I do!" Instead, He simply told them to pray after His example. He taught them how to pray. Jesus wanted His disciples to walk in the same authority and intimacy He had.

There is a secret place where God forms us. There is a place where we are known and where we are empowered to carry His authority. There is a place where we are permitted to approach His throne, to bear our hearts, to seek His help, and to be rewarded by a Father who knows all that we need even before we ask. We all long to find a place where we are known, a place where we belong. Where is that place? What must we do to find it? That secret place is an altar. It is your personal altar.

## What Is an Altar?

An altar is a place of death. It is a place set aside for intentional sacrifice. Throughout the Old Testament, altars were places where God's people offered sacrifices to Him. That tradition of sacrifice eventually came to focus on a bronze altar in the courtyard of the temple. Every day, worshipers brought animals to be sacrificed. During special religious festivals, the number of sacrifices could swell into the thousands, perhaps hundreds of thousands, as it did when Solomon dedicated the temple.

> When all the elders of Israel had arrived, the priests took up the ark, and they brought up the ark of the LORD and the tent of meeting and all the sacred furnishings in it. The priests and Levites carried them up, and King Solomon and the entire assembly of Israel that had gathered about him were before the ark, sacrificing so many sheep and cattle that they could not be recorded or counted.
>
> 1 Kings 8:3–5

Worshipers would bring the best of their unblemished livestock and offer them to God at that altar. These daily sacrifices were an act of worship, but also a personal sacrifice that each worshiper made.

The temple's system of worship must have been an overwhelming thing to witness. It was one of the most spectacular scenes in the ancient world. Who wouldn't have been impressed by the scale of the worship, the gold of the temple's architecture, the massive stones, the giant bronze altar, the crowds of worshipers, and the songs of their praise? But do not miss the central act taking place. At the center of their worship was an act of death—an animal was sacrificed. The altar was the symbolic place of that death.

Why was death so central to Israel's worship? It was because of sin that separates us from God. There was no way to approach God's presence without a sacrifice. At that time, sacrifices were the means of recognizing the consequences of sin and were an image of their willingness to put to death those things that kept them from His presence. It was an act of relationship. The Israelites would sacrifice the best of what they possessed to receive something better from God, His presence and blessing. Sacrifice was the path to God.

This practice of sacrifice prepared God's people for the coming of Jesus, who would be the ultimate and final sacrifice. As it had been with Israel's worship and the temple itself, the center of Jesus' life and obedience was also death, His own death. As the Old Testament prophets had long understood, the blood of bulls and rams could never fully deal with sin. They were an act of hope, a sacrifice that anticipated a better sacrifice to come.

The sacrifice of Jesus demonstrated how much God wanted to be in relationship with His people. "God demonstrates his own love for us in this: While we were still sinners, Christ died for us" (Romans 5:8). Jesus' death did what all of the sacrifices of Israel's history never could: it gave us eternal access to God, and it established a new intimacy with Him. As the author of Hebrews put it, "We have been made holy through the sacrifice of the body of Jesus Christ once for all" (10:10). Jesus was the final sacrifice for sin, and there would be no more temple sacrifices. It wasn't, however, the end of the altar or sacrifice or death.

There is still a required death in order to follow Jesus. We are required to put to death our flesh. We are required to die to ourselves. To receive this new relationship with God, each of us must still die to ourselves. The apostle Paul famously explained, "Therefore, I urge you, brothers and sisters, in view of God's mercy, to offer your bodies as a living sacrifice, holy and pleasing to God—this is your true and proper worship" (Romans 12:1).

We no longer place bulls or rams on a temple altar, but we still make sacrifices. We still worship through death. We now offer our own lives as the sacrifice, a living sacrifice. We offer the death of our will. We build an altar, and we place our lives upon it. You must remember that first and foremost, your personal altar is a place of death to self-will. Entering that secret place with God always requires fresh resubmitting of ourselves to God and His will.

An unwillingness to die to ourselves inevitably stunts our relationship with God, our willingness to pray to Him, and our desire to be with Him. Oftentimes, people fail to pray because they don't know how to say no. They don't know how to put to death the priority of their own calendars, appetites, emotions, and distractions. Every day that you pray, you will make a sacrifice. Every day that sacrifice will be consumed and, the next day, you will do it again. Your life is now a daily living sacrifice. You enter that secret place with God through the altar of putting to death your flesh, your agenda, and your will.

We learn to do that, as the ancient peoples did, through three parts: the part removed, the part shared, and the part consumed.

## The Part Removed

But the hide of the bull and all its flesh, as well as the head and legs, the internal organs and the intestines—that is, all the rest of the bull—he must take outside the camp to a place ceremonially clean, where the ashes are thrown, and burn it there in a wood fire on the ash heap.

Leviticus 4:11–12

The book of Leviticus offers a detailed description of how Israel was to make sacrifices. For the regular sin offerings, they were given specific instructions about the parts of each animal that were to be removed. This was to happen not only at the altar in the temple, but in the entire city or camp. The animal hide, head, legs, and specific organs were to be taken to a clean site outside of the city and burned in a fire of wood. The sacrifice for sin included what was given to God but also this part that was removed and carried away.

As we prepare our lives for daily sacrifice, we often have things that need to be removed. Each day, as we place our lives on the altar, we go about the work of removing what is not pleasing to God.

> As we place our lives on the altar, we go about the work of removing what is not pleasing to God.

We search our hearts for unconfessed sin, for evil desires, unholy motives, and wrong ideas. Often, we discover things in our lives we had not noticed before.

These aren't always just sins, though it certainly includes them. As we grow in our relationship with God, we discover

63

things that distract us from Him and things He finds unpleasing in us. It is a constant process of removal and refinement.

The expectations my wife and I had of our children were different when they were toddlers than when they were teenagers. As they grew, we expected more from them. There were things in their childhood that we expected them to grow out of as young adults. Our parental discipline was based on the child's age and development.

So it is with our heavenly Father. His discipline is not all at once. He walks with us. He expects more of us as we grow and mature in faith. You are in a lifelong process of removing and correcting things in your heart. You are in a lifelong process of growing up in faith and learning to please your heavenly Father. That work is done daily at the altar.

**A lifetime of daily sacrifice changes you.**

I once spoke with a minister who had left the ministry due to a significant moral failure. He shared that it had not been a single moment of temptation that brought him down. He had gone through a long period in which he had daily refused God's warnings.

"How long had God been dealing with you about this?" I asked.

"A long time," he answered. "Eventually, I stopped praying altogether because God kept bringing it up." It's usually that way. God graciously offers to help us remove things in the privacy of our secret place. It is also God's grace that He doesn't give up on us. He pesters us. His heart is to reveal these vulnerabilities before they lead us into sin. But when we neglect this daily work, He is forced to discipline us in public. The consequences can be devastating.

God offers this daily lesson of discipline because He is good to you. God points to something and allows you to recognize that it isn't pleasing to Him. You begin the work of removing that thing from your life, carrying it outside the camp, and leaving it behind. You don't have to do that work on your own. God helps you, but you do have to do it. And where else in this world are you instructed how to say no, how to grow in holiness, how to voluntarily give up things that are holding you back?

You need a daily altar to take up that work. And I want you to see the potential of it. A lifetime of daily sacrifice changes you. It matures you. It grows your relationship with God and the power of the authority you can walk in. Come to this altar each day with a willingness to remove what God demands and you will change. You will grow. You will not be the same person—not tomorrow and certainly not a year from now or a lifetime from now. There are things God wants to remove from your life, and they begin at your altar of sacrifice.

## The Part Shared

> The sin offering is to be slaughtered before the LORD in the place the burnt offering is slaughtered; it is most holy. The priest who offers it shall eat it; it is to be eaten in the sanctuary area, in the courtyard of the tent of meeting.
>
> Leviticus 6:25–27

There is often a second part to a sacrifice. The ancient sacrifices that were offered each day were the means by which the priests survived. Dedicated to serving the Lord, the priests were allowed to eat a portion of the sacrifices. They lived off the sacrifices that others offered. If every Israelite had decided not to sacrifice, the priesthood could not have survived.

It is always that way with sacrifice. As we become a living sacrifice, our life becomes a service to others. We give something of ourselves away to support them, to help them survive. As God removes things from our lives, He also frees us to give and share in ways we weren't previously able. Dying to ourselves means living for others. Being a living sacrifice changes the way we think about our rights, our finances, our desires, and our time. Having placed them on the altar, God is now able to use them in new ways. We tend to think of sacrifices as only something lost, but God uses them to feed and sustain someone else.

A sacrifice frees us from needing to look out for ourselves. We spend much of our time trying to protect what we have and trying to accumulate more. When others make demands of us, expect things from us, or use us in ways we didn't agree to, we often get frustrated and defensive. We push back and start protecting ourselves. But when God reworks our hearts through sacrifice, we begin to see what we have as something to be shared. We give so that others might have. Ultimately, your life is in God's hands to be distributed to others as He sees best.

Jesus understood that He had not come to be served but to serve, to give His life away to others (see Mark 10:45). His sacrifice became our bread of life and cup of salvation. Jesus was able to make that sacrifice not because of some personality type or special gift of hospitality. He could give His life away because He had submitted it fully to His Father. He had sacrificed His will and offered His life to be used by God.

When Jesus asked John to baptize Him, John was reluctant. John understood water baptism as a sign of repentance. He knew who Jesus was. What did Jesus need to repent of? Certainly, it wasn't sin. But Jesus insisted on John baptizing Him. Jesus knew He was about to enter a season of temptation, a wilderness time in which Satan would test His faithfulness to God. Jesus' baptism was a turning away from His divine rights as God. Jesus was baptized as an act of submission, submitting His power, will, and rights to God. He would turn away from self-preservation and offer His life as a sacrifice, the blood and bread by which His people would live. He would give Himself away to the world.

As His followers, we do the same. We place our lives on the altar as an act of submission. We allow God to use us on His terms. We renounce our rights and our will. We make ourselves food for others.

You need an intentional moment to make that commitment each day, to place yourself on the altar and remember again that your life is now His life. You need an intentional act of surrender that frees you to live for others, for Him.

## The Part Consumed

He shall remove all the fat from the bull of the sin offering—all the fat that is connected to the internal organs, both

67

kidneys with the fat on them near the loins, and the long lobe of the liver, which he will remove with the kidneys—just as the fat is removed from the ox sacrificed as a fellowship offering. Then the priest shall burn them on the altar of burnt offering.

Leviticus 4:8–10

While part of the sacrifice was removed and part was shared, the best parts of the sacrifice were to be consumed by fire. They were to be burned so that the aroma would ascend and please God. There are things in your life that need to be removed and things that need to be given to others, but there are also things that God reserves for you and Him alone. You need an altar because you need a daily place to be with God. A place to enjoy His presence and a place to grow in friendship. You need a place to be honest, to struggle, to argue, to confess, to receive, to worship, and to enjoy. It will take cleansing and submission to get there, but there is a secret place God has for you and Him alone. You need a personal altar because it is your access to that secret place with God.

> **You need an altar because it is your access to that secret place with God.**

If that is new to you, I would suggest you spend some time reading Psalm 139. It is a psalm in which David describes his secret place with God. He writes:

> For you created my inmost being;
> you knit me together in my mother's womb.

68

I praise you because I am fearfully and wonderfully
    made;
  your works are wonderful,
  I know that full well.
My frame was not hidden from you
  when I was made in the secret place,
  when I was woven together in the depths of the
    earth.
Your eyes saw my unformed body;
  all the days ordained for me were written in your
    book
  before one of them came to be.
How precious to me are your thoughts, God!
  How vast is the sum of them!
Were I to count them,
  they would outnumber the grains of sand—
  when I awake, I am still with you.

Psalm 139:13–18

Deep within our hearts are some pretty important questions. Who am I? Why am I here? What is my purpose in life? At times, those questions can feel like a curse, even a joke. We can't seem to find answers, at least not meaningful ones. The world tells us to search our heart or to buy some self-help product. But the world doesn't really know how to answer those questions. It is not willing to make the sacrifice necessary to find them. Those are the questions to be answered in our secret place with God. David understood it.

There is a place you were made beyond your mother's womb. There is place in which your identity, your abilities, your image, and your purpose were knit together by the hand of God. It is the place where you were fearfully and wonderfully made. There is something deep within you created by God. Sure, sin and broken humanity sometimes make it hard to recognize, but God has not hidden it from you. He has invited you into it. He offers you His thoughts, His plans, His design for your life. David experienced these secret things in numbers uncountable. God wants to flood you with a sense of His love, purpose, and your true identity. He longs to do it.

As I stated before, I believe altars are a means of connecting heaven and earth. That also means that your personal altar is the place where who you are on earth is connected with that secret, heavenly place in which you were first formed by God.

I have this crazy idea that as we enter heaven and Jesus shows us the place He went ahead to prepare for us, we will recognize it. I think it is that secret place where we were created. That place we have experienced before through prayer and daily showing up at our personal altar. I think for those who pray daily in that secret place, that heavenly mansion will feel instantly like home, a place we have gone to pray each day on earth. It is a place in my life that has long been marked out, where my daily bread has been stored, and where God has met me so many times before.

I believe that David wrote Psalm 139 in his secret place. I think he wrote it sensing who he really was and what he had in God. He wrote it out of a deep, personal, and private relationship with God. He concluded that psalm by writing,

70

"Search me, God, and know my heart; test me and know my anxious thoughts. See if there is any offensive way in me, and lead me in the way everlasting" (verses 23–24). Our way into that place is by praying: *God, search me. Reveal my heart. Test me. Remove anything offensive to You. Lead me into that eternal everlasting place.*

I don't know what waits for you in that secret place, but I know it is good. I know that your church and those you lead depend on you finding it. I know it will require you removing things from your life and submitting things to God you would rather protect and keep for yourself. But if you are willing to build a personal altar, if you're willing to daily lay your life on it, God will meet you there. He will take you to a new place. He will show you things, speak things to you, and pour His love and grace into your life. You will live differently. You will lead differently.

Perhaps you have tried before. Perhaps you have prayed and not made it yet. It doesn't matter. Some days it is discipline and work, some days it is glory upon glory. What matters is that you keep showing up. What matters is that you keep listening, removing, sharing, and sacrificing.

Go into your room, shut the door, and pray to your Father who is in heaven. He will reward you. He is the reward.

## Building the Altar

"I rise before dawn and cry for help; I have put my hope in your word" (Psalm 119:147).

1. **Decide when you will pray.** Most of us live by our calendars. Until prayer makes it into our daily planners, prayer is only a good intention. We all tend to pray when pressure or desperate situations move us to pray, but that isn't a daily altar. You need to fix an appointment with God and keep it. I suggest making prayer your first priority of the morning. Morning prayer reminds us of our need for Him and invites His blessing upon the rest of our day. So, find a time, put it on the calendar, and show up.

2. **Decide where you will pray.** Look for a place away from others where you won't be easily distracted. People often refer to their personal place of prayer as a closet. It describes a place without windows and is usually only large enough for one person. The point is to find a place to which you can daily return. I have a place in the basement of our home where I go each morning. When I travel, I find a spot in my hotel room. I have even made my rental car an altar when it was my only option. Even if you struggle to find an ideal place, don't allow your surroundings to keep you from praying.

3. **Start with the Bible.** The Bible itself reminds us that "in the beginning was the Word" (John 1:1). As part of my responsibilities serving in an executive position with the Assemblies of God, I'm privileged to lead a team of highly qualified content developers working on the Bible Engagement Project. Our research has helped us cultivate ministry partnerships with Barna

72

Research, the American Bible Society, and the Center for Bible Engagement. One of the most important things we've learned from our combined studies is that when a person reads the Bible four or more days a week, it has a greater spiritual impact on them than any other discipline, including regular church attendance.[1]

- If a person engages with the Bible four or more times a week, their likelihood of them giving into temptations such as drinking to excess, viewing pornography, lashing out in anger, gossiping, and lying significantly decrease.

- Receiving, reflecting on, and responding to God's Word four or more times a week decreases a person's odds of struggling with issues such as feeling bitter, thinking destructively about self or others, having difficulty forgiving others, and feeling discouraged.

- Engaging with Scripture produces a more proactive faith among Christians. When a person increases his or her time in Scripture to at least four times a week, the odds of giving financially, memorizing Scripture, and sharing his or her faith with others increases.

- People's perceptions of their own spiritual growth are also impacted by how often they hear from God through the Bible. Those who engage with Scripture most days of the week are

73

less likely to feel spiritually stagnant and to feel that they can't please God.

The powerful effects of Bible engagement on spiritual growth have been reliably demonstrated across many studies. When you pray, there's no better place to start than with the Word of God.

4. **Keep a journal.** When I go to prayer, I often begin by reading from the Bible. I journal what I hear God saying to me through His Word. That experience moves me to pray through worship and with new requests. The Word of God is active and alive and is a powerful guide to prayer (see 2 Timothy 3:16).

5. **Learn to pray the Lord's Prayer.** When Jesus' disciples asked Him to teach them to pray, He offered them the Lord's Prayer. It is a wonderful prayer prompt. Begin by reading the prayer or reciting it from memory. Then slow down and use each phrase as a prompt to pray. Learn to pray for His Kingdom to come. Learn to pray for daily provisions of bread. Learn to pray for His forgiveness and His way of escape from temptation. You can't go wrong with Jesus' prayer as your guide.

# FIVE

# Building the Core Altar

*Aaron and Hur held his hands up—one on one side, one on the other—so that his hands remained steady till sunset. So Joshua overcame the Amalekite army with the sword.*

*Exodus 17:12–13*

What happens on the mountain determines what happens in the valley below. That is one of the most fundamental truths of spiritual leadership I know. Perhaps the second truth is that there is always a cost to stay on that mountain. We are called to lead from the mountain, but we need help to do it.

There are things to which God calls a leader that only that leader can do. Chief among them is prayer. Certainly, the whole church is called to pray, but the leader's authority and intimacy in prayer have an exponential effect on the church.

75

When a leader fails to pray, the whole church feels the impact of that failure. But when a leader dedicates oneself to leading by prayer, that prayer has an impact on the whole church. The importance of prayer cannot be overemphasized when it comes to leading a church or a family forward. All true progress is made by prayer. There is no more important work than prayer. But it can be dangerous and is often exhausting.

The mountaintop is the place where we meet with God, and the valley is the place where the work of ministry is done and the physical resources of the church are administered.

> The importance of prayer cannot be overemphasized when it comes to leading a church forward.

The mountain is the place of spiritual leadership, while the valley is the place of physical work. Leading from the mountain and leading from the valley require very different skill sets and attention. The valley is the place where we construct systems and where we measure resources. It is the place where we give. The mountain is the place where we receive from the presence of God. We need wise and skilled leaders in both, but we cannot allow the pressures of the valley to force us off the mountain. God calls a pastor, leader, and parent to the mountain.

The tension between these two priorities was one of the main challenges the early Church faced in the first century. As the church began to grow, the apostles found themselves giving more time to the physical needs of the community and to the conflicts that rose from those decisions. The book of Acts records that not long after Christ's ascension, the

Church became conflicted over how to provide care to widows (see Acts 6:1–4). It was a logistical question that was also complicated by divisions between Jews and Gentiles.

Certainly, these needs and the growing conflict around them were issues the apostles cared about and were responsible for, but they recognized that their time and energy could be easily distracted. They could end up spending all their time managing these processes and, in doing so, forfeit the work they knew they were called to. Instead of taking up the work themselves, they appointed deacons to take charge. It was an act of delegation and an act of prioritization. The apostles decided to prioritize what they alone could do and what the Church could not afford to lose—prayer.

The apostles explained, "We will turn this responsibility over to them [the new deacons] and will give our attention to prayer and the ministry of the word" (Acts 6:3–4). The apostles delegated work not just to save themselves time and energy but to prioritize praying and preaching the Word. They had been called to lead through prayer, and they could not lose that priority. They chose to stay on the mountain and to appoint skilled leaders to take up the work of the valley.

Pastors who believe it is their job to do the ministry are the lids to their churches. A pastor's job is to send leaders into ministry and to empower the church to do the work among the people. Pastors are called to equip the saints for the work, and they are called to pray and preach the Word. It is easy to think of this as only a logistical reality. For the church to grow, there must be more leaders to serve. While that is true, I also want you to recognize that this principle is also a spiritual reality. For the church to grow and fulfill its purposes, the pastor must maintain his or her priority of prayer and his or her place on the mountain.

### The Potential of a Pastor Who Prays

I love to read about past revivals, and one of the patterns that always emerges is the prioritization of prayer that sustained those seasons of renewal. Revivals are not a consequence of marketing or systems. Revivals happen because a man or woman has an encounter with God and refuses to come down from the mountain. Revivals happen because of the prioritization of prayer.

> Revivals happen because of the prioritization of prayer.

Have you read about the ministry of Jonathan Edwards? Edwards did not have a charismatic personality. Those who heard him preach described his quiet voice and solemn demeanor. Edwards usually read his sermons from carefully written manuscripts, sometimes failing to even look up at those to whom he preached. Edwards was not who you would imagine a revival preacher to be. But Edwards knew how to lead from the mountain. Edwards led many of the revivals that became a part of America's first Great Awakening.

The Spirit moved because Edwards prioritized prayer. He described it as the believer's "great duty,"[1] and he wrote of his own unceasing prayers. "It was always my manner, at

78

such times, to sing forth my contemplations. Prayer seemed to be natural to me; as the breath, by which the inward burnings of my heart had vent."[2]

It is always that way with those who awaken revival. Prayer is a way of living—a way of breathing. Revival happens first in their personal times of prayer, but it spreads as they refuse to come down from the higher place, choosing instead to lead from the mountain. Prayer makes all things possible. It can make the preaching of a bookish and timid minister the burning fire of another Great Awakening. We need pastors who will lead and preach from the repositories of their mountaintop prayer.

Perhaps our best example of leading from the mountain was Moses. Moses had been trained by the Egyptians to be a leader and to excel in battle techniques and government administration. Having also spent so many years in the hardships of the desert and the wilderness, he was certainly capable and skilled. But as the Israelites prepared to face the Amalekites, Moses knew his place was not on the battlefield but on the mountain above (see Exodus 17:8–13).

He appointed Joshua to lead the battle in the valley. And as Joshua prepared the army for that battle, Moses scaled the mountain with his staff. As the two armies collided on the battlefield, Moses raised his hands over the conflict. He was joined by Aaron and Hur. It did not take the soldiers long to recognize that Moses, though physically distant from the battle, was the most important factor in Israel's success.

There was a spiritual battle happening on the mountain just as there was a physical battle taking place below. Exodus records, "As long as Moses held up his hands, the Israelites were winning, but whenever he lowered his hands, the Amalekites were winning" (verse 11). Moses controlled the victory from the mountain. I believe that is one of the Bible's clearest images of leadership. God's leader is called to stand on the mountain and to pray. Those prayers determine the outcome.

Aaron and Hur could see this reality in the physical ebb and flow of battle lines, but it is no less true of our own prayers. When we pray, God's army is moved. When we pray, victory comes. For any leader who is called by God, prayer is the first responsibility. It is not something we do when it is needed—it is our calling and a priority that we refuse to give up.

In the previous chapter, we discussed the gift of prayer as our intimacy with God. Now we must recognize the responsibility of it, too. If you are a leader, you have been called to pray. You have been called to the mountain. So much depends on it. But responsibilities always come with a challenge. The challenge we face in prayer is not only starting to pray but continuing to pray. It is hard to stay on the mountain.

## The Cost of Prayer

Moses understood the importance of his hands staying raised, but that didn't change the difficulty of the task. Moses grew tired. His arms grew tired. At some point they must have begun to fall, and they watched as the consequences played out on the battlefield below them. The Israelites began to lose. Moses wanted to keep them raised, but he grew weary—as we also do.

You can understand the responsibility of prayer and still find it difficult to sustain the work. You can know what God offers on the mountain and still find yourself sliding back into the valley. If you are going to sustain your prayers, you need to recognize it will be a battle.

Prayer always requires personal sacrifice. It requires time, but it also causes pain and requires endurance. Moses experienced that responsibility in the form of physical pain and weakness. Anyone who prays eventually pays a cost. Spiritual battles always become physical ones. Daniel first began a battle in heaven and then ended up in a very physical lion's den. If you pray, things will change. As they change, you will feel it personally. The enemy fears most the power of prayer because it is always the spiritual battle that matters most. But to win the battle, we must also fight the natural battle and its many temptations.

I have heard many people who, having committed to a new intensity of prayer, later admit that things were easier before they began to pray. We pray and suddenly find all sorts of things going wrong. That shouldn't surprise you. When you pray, you are doing something dangerous. You are doing something that matters. The prayers of a pastor often change the spiritual atmosphere and expose tensions, division, and sin. Prayer often leads to conflict and persecution.

Prayer changes things, and change always produces resistance. The enemy is content to let us stay busy with ministry, but when we begin to pray, we initiate a spiritual battle. There are always counterattacks. There will be a temptation to let up and avoid the pain.

There is also the temptation of distraction. As our prayers begin to expose problems and sins, we want to get busy fixing things. That's what we have been trained to do. We shift our attention from prayer and start taking up these new challenges and newly exposed problems. This is the same temptation the apostles first faced—give up some prayer time to work on the church's systems of support. But the more we pray, the more we must focus and delegate.

You can also count on facing the criticism of others. Those who do not value prayer have a hard time recognizing the value of prayer in the life of their pastor. People will see it as a waste of time. They will offer endless opinions about how you should be spending your time and about what they expect you to accomplish. It is easy to leave the hill if you are trying to appease those who criticize the time you spend there.

But perhaps the greatest temptation is weariness. Moses grew tired. We do, too. Prayer and the spiritual battles that prayer awakens make us tired. There is always a weariness to prayer. We carry a heavy burden and bear a great responsibility. Jesus often withdrew to pray, and He experienced the burden of it. He prayed with tears and with drops of blood (see Luke 22:44).

Do you remember when Jesus asked His disciples to pray with Him in the Garden of Gethsemane? They kept falling asleep (see Luke 22:45–46). I think they understood the gravity of the moment, but it was hard to sustain such a weight.

It wears us out. Who hasn't become distracted or even dozed off in prayer? Sustained prayer is an act of spiritual endurance. And it is in these moments of weariness that we need the help of others.

The reason every pastor needs a core team of prayer partners is because we are weak and tire easily. We, like Moses, begin to lose our posture. Our hands begin to fall, and we risk losing the battle. Thankfully, Moses wasn't alone on that mountain. Seeing his hands beginning to slip, "they took a stone and put it under him and he sat on it. Aaron and Hur held his hands up— one on one side, one on the other—so that his hands remained steady till sunset" (Exodus 17:12). Moses did not pray alone. He was surrounded by those who were willing to lift him up. He was surrounded by those who held him accountable to prayer. That stone beneath him was an altar, an altar in which prayer partners helped him sustain the spiritual battle of prayer.

> You need a core team of partners who will join you and sustain you in prayer.

I have been blessed to have had similar partners in prayer throughout my ministry. The work I have endeavored has depended on them. I would not take up the work of ministry without ensuring I had prayer partners joining me. I believe in the power of prayer more than I believe in the gravity that holds me to the ground. But I, too, have grown tired. As I surrounded myself with prayer partners, I began to feel a new level of accountability. Some days I showed up to pray because I knew they were praying for me, and I knew they were counting on me to pray for them. I didn't want to let them down. They reminded me of what mattered most, and they kept me praying when my own strength faltered.

I think God honors their partnership and prayers as much as my own, just as God honored Moses' hands that were held up by Aaron and Hur. On my best days, I come to prayer energized and passionate. But even on the days that I feel weary, because of their support, I still show up and pray. God honors that, too. You need a core team of partners who will join you and sustain you in prayer. You need their accountability and their help.

### Partners in Prayer

Most pastors will be familiar with the work of John Maxwell. His leadership books have helped millions lead at a higher level. Certainly, I have learned much from him and am a better leader thanks to his work. But perhaps one of my favorite Maxwell books is one of his least known. Early in Maxwell's career, he wrote a book titled *Partners in Prayer*. The book is dedicated to the importance of supporting a pastor through prayer. From the beginning, Maxwell understood that prayer was critical to spiritual leadership.

Maxwell writes:

God's hand moves when people and pastors pray together. . . . I can personally attest to the benefits that others' prayers have given me. There have been times when I've gotten ready to do a service or conference, and I've been physically exhausted. But when my prayer partners lay hands on me, and I see them praying over the auditorium, I receive a new strength—physically, mentally, spiritually, and emotionally. I feel prepared to receive the power of God.[3]

That is my prayer for you as well. I pray that you find partners who will pray with you, pray for you, and keep you praying. C. Peter Wagner wrote, "The most underutilized source of spiritual power in our churches today is intercession for Christian leaders."[4] I couldn't agree more.

So how do you go about forming such a group of prayer partners? Once again, Moses is a good place to start. Moses had Aaron and Hur. I think they represent the kinds of partnerships we need in ministry.

We know quite a bit about Aaron. Aaron served as the first priest in Israel's history. Aaron was a minister and,

> The best way to find a partner in prayer is to look for the people around you who are already praying.

like Moses, was dedicated to full time ministry work. Aaron had long been a partner with Moses and knew him personally. He certainly understood Moses' history, as well as his struggles, frustrations, and vulnerabilities. Aaron supported Moses as a fellow minister in the work.

We each need ministry partners who understand us and the work we are doing. We need fellow ministers to join with us in prayer. These ministry prayer partnerships often form outside of the churches we lead. If you are a pastor, look around and find another pastor with whom you can pray and with whom you can share accountability. Pray together and share the needs you're facing. Share the challenges of prayer, and bear some of that weight together.

We know less about Hur than we do Aaron. Hur was most likely a lay Israelite. Perhaps Hur was an administrative leader or a craftsman. Hur reminds us that you don't have to be a religious leader to be a partner in prayer. Hur may simply have been a friend who understood the weight Moses carried and was willing to help share that load. Some of my greatest partners in prayer have been men in the churches I serve. They are men of various ages and professions, but all are passionate about and are dedicated to prayer.

The best way to find a partner in prayer is to look for the people around you who are already praying. Perhaps they are other pastors; perhaps they are congregants. Look for those who are already committed to prayer and invite them to pray with you. (I recommend you find someone of the same gender.) Set regular times to pray together.

Also, share the task of prayer with others in your church. Sometimes it is as simple as asking them to pray for you. Ask them to pray over your services. Ask them to pray for God's anointing on your prayers and preaching. Sometimes all you need to do is ask. And if you are a member of a church, let the pastors know that you're praying for them. Let them know you are willing to help bear the responsibility of lifting them up in prayer.

I mentioned previously that Jesus took His disciples with Him to pray in the Garden of Gethsemane. Jesus often did that. He took His disciples with Him when He withdrew to pray. He took Peter, James, and John with Him to the Mount of Transfiguration. Jesus was teaching them how to pray, but He also asked them to pray with Him. Jesus dedicated intentional time—an altar—for praying with others. If He needed partners in prayer, then we surely do, too. We lead best from the mountain when we are surrounded by faithful partners dedicated to keeping us there.

C. H. Spurgeon put it well: "Whenever God determines to do a great work, He first sets His people to pray."[5] Our victories in the value come when we take the time to build an altar of prayer partners to help us sustain our priority of prayer.

## Building the Altar

"Carry each other's burdens, and in this way you fulfill the law of Christ" (Galatians 6:2).

1. **Identify those around you who are already praying.** We all need others to support us in prayer, but prayer partnership takes intentionality. You are going to have to build the kind of relationships with people who will stand with you in prayer. Begin by looking at the people around you who are already praying. Who do you know that believes in prayer and already has his or her own prayer altar? Identify the people of prayer God has already placed in your life.

2. **Ask them to join you in prayer.** Sometimes, all we need to do is ask. Once you have recognized

individuals who are passionate about prayer, ask them if they would be willing to pray with you. Ask them if they would be willing to join you as a partner in prayer. Be intentional about asking them to bear this responsibility with you. The act of asking helps establish accountability and intentionality. Keep a list of people who have agreed to partner with you in prayer.

3. **Share your prayer needs.** Develop a regular rhythm of communicating your prayer needs to those who have committed to praying with you. Use whatever means is convenient for your group, including in person, over the phone, by email, and via group texting by phone or app. Prayer partnership is only as effective as your willingness to share needs and call one another to prayer. Don't wait until an emergency or crisis. Regularly find things you can pray about.

4. **Find a regular time to pray together.** Though you can pray for one another in your personal times of prayer, there is nothing like praying together in person. Video conferencing is another way to meet if gathering in person does not work. Schedule a time once a week or once a month to pray together. Pray for specific needs, but also take time to allow the Spirit to speak to you and lead you in prayer. You can also schedule special prayer times when you need discernment or are facing a unique challenge.

# SIX

# Building the Community Altar

*When they heard this, they raised their voices together in prayer to God. . . . After they prayed, the place where they were meeting was shaken. And they were all filled with the Holy Spirit and spoke the word of God boldly.*

*Acts 4:24, 31*

We have seen what a single person can do in prayer. We have seen how Daniel defied the world and shook the heavens, and we have seen how the prayers of a leader can have an impact on both the spiritual climate of his or her church, home, and community. We have focused, so far, primarily on individual prayers. There is a secret place with God, a time of hidden prayer, to which each individual believer is called, but we are not

89

always supposed to pray alone. There is also a time when we are to pray together. There is an altar where a community of believers join together in agreement. An altar where we combine our voices and find our prayers amplified before God. I want to show you why praying together is so important and how your church can learn to do it.

If you read through the stories of the first days of the Church, there are some obvious patterns you will notice. Certainly, you will recognize the way they went into the world proclaiming the Gospel, but perhaps even more prominent than their preaching was their praying. And they did much of that praying together. In chapter after chapter of Acts, the Church was gathered in prayer. They prayed when there was cause for celebration, when they faced opposition, and in the normal rhythms and routines of everyday life. The early Church was constantly praying, and they were doing it together. The early Church was a community of prayer.

**The first collective act of the Church was praying together.**

After Jesus' ascension, a small group of His believers met in the Upper Room to pray. As Jesus had commanded them, they prayed until they received the Holy Spirit and the boldness that came with Him. Before they turned the world upside down with their preaching and miracles, they prayed for the power to do it. The first collective act of the Church was praying together. And it didn't stop. That pattern of prayer only continued.

In the very next chapter, we encounter Peter and John going up to the temple during the hour of prayer. Even after

Jesus had ascended and the Spirit had fallen in that Upper Room, the Church stayed committed to a regular time of prayer in the temple. Just as Daniel continued to kneel daily at his window to pray, so, too, the Church continued going daily to the temple to pray. Their commitment to pray together wasn't sporadic. They had a regular time and place for it.

When the chief priest and the temple leadership began to threaten Peter and John, warning them to stop speaking about Jesus, the two men returned to the Church with the message. How did they respond to these new threats? They prayed. Acts records, "Peter and John went back to their own people and reported all that the chief priests and the elders had said to them. When they heard this, they raised their voices together in prayer to God" (Acts 4:23–24).

That is the picture Acts consistently paints of the Church. They sang hymns, they broke bread, and they studied Scripture, but nothing was more central or consistent than their raised voices of prayer. The Church praying together is the driving force of the book of Acts.

Why did they do it? Why did they so consistently turn to prayer? They prayed because they had witnessed firsthand the power of their collective prayers. As they began to pray against the demonic threats that sought to keep them quiet, Acts says the room where they prayed was powerfully stirred. "After they prayed, the place where they were meeting was shaken. And they were all filled with the Holy Spirit and spoke the word of God boldly" (Acts 4:31).

If you want to know what made the early Church so effective, if you want to know how they changed the world, how they witnessed the miraculous, how they boldly preached before kings and beggars, and why they sacrificed their lives, the answer is simple: they had a regular and prioritized practice of prayer that shook the earth and empowered them with supernatural boldness to keep on speaking. It all comes back to prayer.

Something dynamic happens when we pray together. It is that simple. God hears every prayer, and Christ intercedes on behalf of every believer—even those who pray silently or in isolation, but Scripture shows us that the authority of our prayers is multiplied when we join together. As Jesus reminded us, "For where two or three gather in my name, there am I with them" (Matthew 18:20).

For as often as Jesus prayed alone, He also joined with His disciples in prayer and participated in the regular prayers of the temple and the festivals. It was Jesus who reminded Jerusalem that the temple itself was a house of prayer, a place in which all followers of God came together to pray.

## The Church's Lost Priority of Prayer

The consistency of community prayer is so prominent throughout Scripture that it is hard to overstate its priority. The Church is not the Church without prayer. Yet how many believers today go through life never learning or practicing communal prayer, never becoming confident enough to raise their voice with others? We might listen to other people pray, we might close our eyes together, or we might add "amen" at the end of a prayer, but how many people really know how to agree together in prayer? Perhaps the prophetic weakness of today's Church and the fear we have of sharing our faith reflects our diminished practice of prayer. For when the Church prays, the house is always shaken, and the people are always emboldened. The Church needs believers who know how to pray alone as well as how to pray together.

It is my experience that most individuals tend to be drawn to either personal or corporate prayer. Perhaps it is connected to our individual personality traits, perhaps something about being introverted or extroverted. Many find it quite natural to pray in private but may struggle to publicly add their voice to the corporate time of prayer. Others may pray publicly with boldness and even volume but struggle to make a private practice of prayer consistent. It is easy to develop ruts and fall back into what comes easiest for each of us. But that is not how the Bible presents prayer.

Prayer is not about what makes us comfortable or what best fits our personality. We are all called to pray both in private and together. That will certainly mean moments of challenging ourselves and stretching beyond our own comfort, but we can't afford not to.

And it can be learned. Praying is not a personality type, praying is a responsibility we accept as God's people, His ambassadors on earth. We don't learn to do anything well without regularly practicing it. You won't wake up and find that you are suddenly experienced at prayer. And your church won't suddenly become dynamic at it, either. It takes a willingness to learn and grow. It takes leadership and regular intentional effort.

As our lives have become more complicated and our church participation minimized, there are simply fewer chances for us to pray together. It is hard to discern a specific pattern of prayer in the early Church because it seems almost constant. There were daily times of prayer in the temple, evening prayers in homes, and stretches of prayer in which they didn't leave until something happened. Prayer was far more than a single segment of a weekend service. The Church was prayer. Their lives were immersed in it. It's what they did.

If you are going to build a culture of prayer in your church, if you're going to experience the power of the Spirit at work in your people, prayer must become more than what many churches are used to. You must find ways to practice it. You must find ways to work it into not only your services but into the life of your church. It matters more than you may realize.

Here is why this practice of prayer is so important. There are things that cannot be done without a regular place of prayer. It is a truth given to us by Jesus Himself. One of Jesus' own disciples had to learn this principle in a difficult and embarrassing way.

While Jesus was transfigured on the mountain before Peter, James, and John, the rest of His disciples were trying to cast a reluctant demon out of a young boy. They had done it before. They had cast out plenty of demons on their own. This time, however, things went wrong. What they had done before just didn't work. They couldn't seem to drive this particular demon out.

As Jesus came down from the mountain, He found them with the boy and the boy's father. Apparently, the boy's manifestations must have drawn the attention of those around, because a crowd had formed. The father's words are so sad to read. He told Jesus of the boy's seizures and how the demon constantly cast him into fires and into the water. In a poignant statement, the father admitted, "I asked your disciples to drive out the spirit, but they could not" (Mark 9:18).

As a father myself, I can feel the pain and sorrow of the burden this father carries. He was desperate, and the disciples, who I imagine said they could help, could not. Jesus cast the demon out with a single command.

Later in private, the disciples asked Jesus for an explanation. Why couldn't they cast the demon out? Jesus explained to them, "This kind can come out only by prayer" (Mark 9:29). It is a remarkable statement. Jesus seems to indicate that there are certain demonic powers and forces that require a particular kind of prayer if they are going to be driven out. Jesus' language is also interesting. What the King James Version translates as "prayer and fasting" is actually a single word in the Greek. It often describes a place of prayer, a recurring discipline of prayer practiced in a particular place.

> There are things that simply cannot be done without a regular commitment to praying together.

Certainly, the disciples knew how to pray, but Jesus suggests that there are certain demonic forces that can only be driven out by a consistent place of prayer. It may be that the kind of devils that are now present in America are the same kind of devils Jesus was speaking of. This present manifestation of evil is of a kind we have never faced before, and it will require a different kind of prayer to defeat it. Better preaching and music, more saturated calendars of activities, more fellowships and fundraisers will not affect them. A new level of prayer is required when there is a new level of devil.

This is what so many churches are missing. They might know how to pray. They may even pray individually at home. But they do not have a recurring regular place of prayer in which the Spirit is given opportunity to drive out the most entrenched forces of darkness. There are things that simply cannot be done without a regular commitment to praying together. Jesus and His followers have long understood that. It is a truth the Church today cannot afford to continue ignoring.

### Learning to Pray Together

What does the Church do when it prays together? Ask a group of believers to gather in prayer and most will begin with prayer requests. What can we pray about? Who should we be praying for? Who is sick? Who is facing a personal crisis? There is nothing wrong with praying for these needs. Scripture encourages us to lift our needs and pray for one another. It's important to pray *for* people, but we are also called to pray the Kingdom *forward*.

*The whole Church was shaken and empowered.*

96

After having been warned to cease speaking about Jesus, the early Church began to cry out to God in prayer. They collectively raised their voices to Him. What were they praying for? It wasn't an individual need. What they prayed for was the advancement of the Gospel despite the world's hostility and the threats of its rulers. Remarkably, they left us an account of the prayer they prayed. Acts records:

> "Sovereign Lord," they said, "you made the heavens and the earth and the sea, and everything in them. You spoke by the Holy Spirit through the mouth of your servant, our father David: 'Why do the nations rage and the peoples plot in vain? The kings of the earth rise up and the rulers band together against the Lord and against his anointed one.' Indeed Herod and Pontius Pilate met together with the Gentiles and the people of Israel in this city to conspire against your holy servant Jesus, whom you anointed. They did what your power and will had decided beforehand should happen. Now, Lord, consider their threats and enable your servants to speak your word with great boldness. Stretch out your hand to heal and perform signs and wonders through the name of your holy servant Jesus."
>
> Acts 4:24–30

Do you recognize their model for corporate prayer? The Church prayed for great boldness and for a move of the Spirit that would unleash healing, signs, and wonders across the city. They were praying for the advancement of God's Kingdom. They prayed for it in the name of Jesus. They also prayed the promises of God from Scripture. They quoted from Psalm 2, acknowledging the way the powers of this world had long opposed the things of God. They connected Scripture and the promises of God with their own day and requested the same miraculous interventions God had done before. Their model of prayer was for the Kingdom to move forward based on the promises of God in Scripture.

What came of their prayers? First, the house where they prayed was shaken. The Kingdom was moved on earth as it was in heaven. Second, Acts tells us they left with supernatural boldness. They were changed. This answer to prayer was not simply an individual's need being met, although that for us is often an area of focus. In this instance, the whole Church was changed. The whole Church was shaken and empowered. And so, too, was their city. Miracles happened. Signs and wonders came. The name of Jesus was proclaimed with power. And for all their attempts, the rulers could not keep them quiet.

This is what the Church needs. It is what your city needs, too. It is what our nation and the whole world needs. We need a move of the Spirit and the bold witness of the Church. But that doesn't come through workshops or conversational techniques. It doesn't come by workflows or pipelines. You can't buy it or program it. All you can do is pray and pray until it comes. Your city will be changed, and your people emboldened when they learn to pray together.

## Leading a Prayer Service

When I teach on prayer and help pastors reprioritize it in their congregations, one of the questions I often hear is, "How can I grow in leading corporate prayer?" Often our churches fail to pray simply because we don't know how to lead them into it. But just as a congregation can grow in prayer, you can grow in your ability to lead your people to pray.

This is one of the reasons I have previously spent so much time describing the priority of personal prayer in the life of a leader. You cannot lead others into prayer if you don't know how to do it on your own. Your ability to lead in prayer is directly connected to your personal discipline of prayer. No advice I give on leading corporate prayer is a replacement for your own prayer life. There is no way to shortcut praying, and there is no technique that is a replacement for a genuine desire to be with God. That must always come first. But there are things we can learn from the prayers of the early Church and how they went about praying together.

> There is power when we agree with one another, but that power takes on supernatural power when we agree together with God's promises.

Acts 4 not only demonstrates the power of praying together, but it also gives us a model for how to do it. When the Church prayed, they did so based on Scripture and the promises of God. You can see it in the prayer I previously quoted. The early Church prayed the Kingdom forward and pushed back the darkness around them. They began by recognizing a place of opposition—a place where the Kingdom needed to move forward—and then they appealed to the promises of God in Scripture to intervene.

If you find yourself before your congregation but are unsure of what to pray about, or perhaps you find yourself running out of things to pray, take heart. You have the accumulated prayers of generations of believers recorded in the Bible to emulate. Use them. Go through Scripture and make a list of the things for which God's people have previously prayed. You'll find plenty to pray about. I keep a list of the prayers I come across in Scripture, and I often use it to help lead prayer services. My list includes things such as

- political leaders
- church leaders
- laborers for the harvest
- boldness to proclaim the Gospel
- signs, wonders, and miracles
- an outpouring of the Holy Spirit
- protection from evil and those who oppose us
- healing for those who are sick

What matters is that you begin accumulating your own scriptural prayer focuses. As you use these topics to lead your congregation into prayer, you may struggle to know how to pray for them. If you have that problem, you can again use Scripture. Find the places in Scripture where God offers corresponding promises to these needs. Lead your people in praying these promises. There is power when we agree with one another, but that power takes on supernatural power when we agree together with God's promises. He then adds

His agreement to ours. In the Bible, you have everything you need to pray and lead in prayer.

There are plenty of things to pray for, but really what you need most is a place to do it and the discipline to do it together. You need an intentional place of praying as a community. You need an old school prayer meeting, a place to tarry, a place to cry out to God, and a place to join together and pray forward the Kingdom of God. Remember, Jesus Himself said there are things that can't be done without a regular place of prayer.

If you are a pastor, creating that place of community prayer is a part of your spiritual responsibility. Without it, your church and city are vulnerable. If you will not do it, you limit what God can do in your people. You must call them to prayer. You must lead them into prayer. And you must make it a regular part of your life together as a church.

Teach your people why prayer matters. Teach them why it matters to pray together. Help them learn to recognize that prayer is the most important thing a church does, that by prayer all other things become possible. Dedicate at least one service a week to praying together. Ask for commitments. We ask people to commit to tithing and volunteering; a commitment to prayer should be at the top of that list.

It will take intentional effort to begin this place of prayer, but in my experience, once established it will become the center of your church and the most important time your church spends together. It will lead you into new boldness and into the miraculous presence of God. As it does, your people will begin to experience the power of prayer for themselves.

Their commitment will grow. Their faith will grow. Their prayer lives will grow.

It all begins with your responsibility to build the altar. Create a place where your people can regularly come and learn to pray together and experience the power of God, the house shaken, and the empowerment of His presence. When we pray together, no darkness can stand against us.

## Building the Altar

"For where two or three are gathered together in my name, there I am with them" (Matthew 18:20).

1. **Participate in or begin a regular prayer service.** For all of the activities that the church generates or participates in, I find that fewer churches regularly meet to pray together. If your church already has a prayer service, make sure you are faithful to attend. If your church does not meet regularly for prayer, perhaps you could start a prayer gathering. You can start with your prayer partners, and then invite the congregation to join you. Your church needs a regular place and time to come together to pray.

2. **Search the Bible for things to pray about.** One thing that can keep you from praying is not knowing what to pray for. I recommend you keep a list of prayers that you find in the Bible. The Bible is full of the prayers of God's people. Pay attention to what they

were praying for. What does the Bible specifically encourage us to pray about? You can use this list of prayers as prompts for leading your prayer service.

3. **Practice praying out loud.** Many people feel intimidated to pray. But like many new things, by practice we become more comfortable. Hearing a church pray out loud builds our faith. It encourages us to lift our own voices to God. As we fill the room with the sounds of prayer, our faith grows. I love the sound of God's people praying, and I believe it is a mark of a healthy church.

4. **Be open to the Spirit.** One of the Spirit's many gifts is leading our prayers. God will guide us and instruct us on how to pray. The Spirit will lead us to prayers we might not have recognized on our own. Come prepared with a list of prayer prompts, but always be sensitive to where the Spirit is leading. As I pray, I often sense the Spirit leading me in new directions. It is true in private prayer, and it is true when we pray together.

# SEVEN

# Building the Miracle Altar

*My message and my preaching were not with wise and persuasive words, but with a demonstration of the Spirit's power, so that your faith might not rest on human wisdom, but on God's power.*

*1 Corinthians 2:4–5*

I had to decide if I had the faith to speak what I heard God saying. What I heard Him saying was that He was present to heal every person in the room. It was a Sunday morning, and I was on the platform ready to move the service from our time of worship through music into the sermon I had spent the week preparing. There was a message of tongues from the congregation, and we all sensed that God had other plans for the service. As we waited for the interpretation, I felt the Spirit prompt me to speak.

When I stepped to the microphone and began to interpret, I didn't know all that God was going to say. As I spoke, the Spirit led me to conclude with the words, "I am present to heal." I understood that God was offering to heal every person in the room. I paused and wondered if I had the faith to say it.

Finally, I explained to the congregation, "You folks know how much I love you, and at times I can speak out of that love and my desire for God to do good things in your life. Sometimes I may speak my desire and not God's. In this instance, I think God is telling me that He wants to heal every person in this room."

I invited anyone who needed healing to come forward. I felt the Lord impress upon me to pray individually for every person who came. I was supposed to lay my hands on every one of them according to Scripture (see James 5:14). I watched as the congregation began to move to the altars. They sensed the same stirring of the Spirit I had. I began laying my hands on and praying for each one.

As I prayed, rows of people began to flood the floor and up onto the platform. Some fell under the power of the Spirit, others wept, and some shouted out the healing they were receiving. We heard countless stories of healing from that day, but a specific one stuck with me.

A young woman came forward with her husband. She looked pregnant. I asked how I could pray, and she explained that although she looked pregnant, she was not. She had been experiencing rapid abdominal growth, and she had no idea what was causing it. She began to weep. With her permission, I put my hand on her stomach to pray. In that moment, the Spirit rushed over her, and the growth collapsed under my hand. Her stomach went flat in a moment. Her husband and the prayer team praying with me all witnessed it. It was gone. She was healed.

I had read in the Bible perhaps more than a hundred times the story of the paralytic who was healed by Jesus (see Luke 5:17–26). Along with that story is Luke's explanation that the power of the Lord had been present for Jesus to heal the sick. I had seen God heal before. But on that day, we all experienced it. We experienced His presence to heal anyone who needed it. God was present to heal us.

That service reminded me of the power of healing and the importance of making space for it. We need an altar, a place where we pray for the miraculous. It has never been more important. God uses miracles to validate His Gospel and, as pastors, we are given the responsibility of administering healing through the authority of our position. God, by His grace, allows us to be participants in it, but we must make the space.

## The Message and Miracles

The early Church was relentless in preaching the Gospel, but not by words alone. They did not depend on clever catch-phrases or marketing slogans. The Gospel was validated by signs and wonders, by the miraculous. When Paul could not get to the sick, he blessed pieces of cloth, causing them to possess the power to heal (see Acts 19:11–12). Peter's preach-ing was affirmed by the miraculous power of even his shadow (see Acts 5:15). The disciples did as Jesus had done. They found the lame and the blind along the roads and pools and offered the power of the Spirit for their healing. Even dramatic events like the death of Ananias and Sapphira made the truth that God's power was alive and active obvious (see Acts 5:1–11). His truth was on public display.

The miracles came not only as blessings to those in need, but also so that the message would be credible. The world in which the early Church preached the Gospel was awash with philosophies and theological ideas. Every city had its teachers and religious authorities. The Roman Empire had become a melting pot of ideas that were sourced from all over the known world. It was not unlike our own day in which truth is left for every individual to decide, and every individual has access to countless truths from which they can choose.

> God often does miracles, not only to heal our physical blindness, but also to heal our spiritual blindness.

When we preach the Gospel, our hearers are forced to weigh its validity against all the other messages they are receiving from social media, news organizations, and their friends and family. It is a confusing and difficult time for people to be able to recognize truth. Perhaps this challenge is made even more difficult by a world that considers the Gospel either offensive or foolish. Our darkened hearts and minds are not predisposed to recognize what is true. So it is that God often does miracles, not only to heal our physical blindness, but also to heal our spiritual blindness. God does the miraculous to validate His truth that the world fights desperately to cover up.

It wasn't just Jesus' preaching that was validated by the miraculous. The intervention of divine miracles is a consistent theme of God's presence, from Genesis to Revelation. Moses was given credibility by the miracles of God, as were Elijah, Elisha, Peter, Stephen, Paul, and countless more. The signs and wonders they performed by the power of the Spirit forced the world to hear the prophetic words of their witness.

Like them, we still bear the heavenly mandate to proclaim the Good News of God's salvation, and like their time, the powers and principalities of this world are working to silence and obscure that truth. So, why should we expect God's miracles to have ceased? Wherever His truth is proclaimed, He is present to heal. He is present to affirm our preaching through the power of miracles. If His Gospel is for today, then His miraculous power is for today as well.

We are what has changed. It is our faith and expectations that have ceased—not His gifts. We fear that we will look foolish. We fear that we might be wrong. We would rather appear wise and weak by the world's standards than foolish and full of the Spirit's power; therefore, we hold back and depend on our cleverness and charisma. We trust our enticing speech to lead people to Christ instead of the powerful hand of God. We trust our words more than His Spirit. We are trying to do with words what God wants to do through miracles.

When Jesus promised that the Holy Spirit would come to us in power, was He predicting clever and well-articulated sermons? I think He had a lot more in mind. I think He was predicting powerful preaching made more powerful by the confirmation of signs and wonders. The apostle Paul reminded the Corinthians that this was also his approach. "My message and my preaching were not with wise and persuasive words, but with a demonstration of the Spirit's power, so that your faith might not rest on human wisdom, but on God's power" (1 Corinthians 2:4–5).

The bottom line is that God does miracles. He always has. He just needs a people and a place—an altar—where He can put them on display.

## The Elders and the Laying on of Hands

How do we go about building an altar for the miraculous? Jesus often gave specific instructions for healing. To one He commanded, "go wash." To another He mixed mud and placed it over his eyes. Jesus told some to go home where their miracle would be waiting for them. Often the miraculous took an intentional act of faith from the recipient. But we aren't left wondering what steps we should take. Scripture gives us very specific instructions about how to pray for healing. Jesus promised we would place our hands on the sick and they would get well. James took Jesus' words seriously and gave us the instruction:

> Is anyone among you sick? Let them call the elders of the church to pray over them and anoint them with oil in the name of the Lord. And the prayer offered in faith will make the sick person well; the Lord will raise them up.

> James 5:14–15

110

One of the themes found throughout Scripture to which I often find myself returning has been one of the central threads of this book. As a pastor, you carry a special spiritual authority. Your prayers have an impact on the church you lead. Your spiritual life sets the pace for the congregation. And your faithfulness to be obedient to this command of Scripture has an impact on the healing your people will experience. God calls the leaders of the church to pray for healing. Healing flows through authority. Why do we see so few healed in the church today? Often it is because we don't practice what Jesus commanded.

The laying on of hands is a symbol of conferring power. The elders of the church are those who have been entrusted with the message of the Gospel. They bear spiritual responsibility for the congregation and with it the authority vested in them by Christ Himself. So, God has designed the power of the Spirit to work through the preaching of His Word and the authority of those entrusted with it.

We have this authority not because we possess some secret prayer or because we have a special power. Scripture is clear that the power to heal has been bought by the blood of Christ. It is by His stripes we are healed. Healing is a part of the atonement and a part of the Gospel's promise. Elders are called to place their hands on the sick as a conduit of authority, as a sign of Christ's Church distributing what Christ purchased.

How many times have I demonstrated a new believer's proclamation of faith by practicing the symbol of baptism: lowering them into the water and bringing them up into that new resurrected life? How many times have I blessed and distributed the symbolic body and blood of Christ that teaches us to anticipate His return? How many weddings have I performed in which I stood and pronounced the new union of a couple, two flesh becoming one? How many new ministers have I placed my hands on and confirmed their ordination to ministry? I do all these things by the power and authority God has given me as a minister. And so, I am also called to lay my hands on the sick, and by that same authority, offer healing.

What do we communicate to Christ's Church if we know He has bought our healing by His own blood but we are reluctant to say it, to offer it? Christ has offered us this great gift, and He commanded us as His representatives to distribute it to the Church. Yet we often find ourselves reluctant and afraid to do it. We risk undermining the Gospel and weakening the faith of others.

> When you neglect this specific work commanded in Scripture, you sever God's power as He intended it to flow.

When you neglect this specific work commanded in Scripture, you sever God's power as He intended it to flow. Perhaps we do not see miracles or healing because we do not pray for them as God instructed us to pray.

Ask yourself a simple question: Are you creating an opportunity for your people to receive their healing? Are you building this altar where the elders of your church, in obedience to God's Word, meet with people to lay their hands on them and anoint them with oil?

When I was a young youth pastor, I had a great pastoral mentor who operated in the gifts of the Spirit and truly understood the power of God's authority rightly administered by a pastor. One Sunday, I was standing in the altar with him praying for the sick. As Scripture commanded, he was placing his hands on each, anointing them with oil, and speaking a prayer of healing over them by faith. I watched as an old man who appeared to be very sick stepped forward for his turn.

I was shocked when my pastor asked him, "Where do you pay your tithes?" The old man explained that he paid tithes to a ministry he liked to watch on television. The pastor explained, "Well then you need to have that ministry lay hands on you and pray for your healing." He went on to explain that this old man was not living under the authority of our church. He would be happy to pray for him and for his healing, but if he really wanted what Scripture had promised, then he needed to be faithful to the submission God had also asked of him.

I listened and thought, *I have never heard anything like this, not in an altar of prayer for the sick.* At our next staff meeting, I brought it up. My pastor kindly explained, "Son, you don't understand the flow of God. I'm submitted to God, and each person in this church must submit to Him, too. God works through authority and our submission to it." He understood the significance of laying on hands, and he had the faith to really practice it.

Two weeks later, the old man showed back up. He explained to us, "I've been paying my tithes here. You are my pastor and I want to submit to the elders of this church."

113

We laid hands on him, and that morning God healed him as well as taught me a valuable lesson.

Authority and submission matter. Each of us must ask ourselves a simple question: Are we willing to submit to what God has asked of us? For the sick, it is submission to the church and its elders. And to you as the pastor, it is submission to the work of laying on hands, anointing with oil, and praying for God's healing.

## The Work Is the Altar

If you are a pastor, God has given you authority, and He has asked you to submit to His way of working through the laying on of hands. Are you willing to submit to what God has asked you to do? Sure, there are times you might be afraid. There are times you may have your doubts. But it isn't your power that heals people, it is your obedience. It is your willingness, by faith, to submit to the call on your life and to operate in the authority God has given you.

So, do it by faith. Do it expecting God to act. Do it with the confidence of the Spirit at work within you. Do it by the promise of God over you. Do it believing that God's authority flows through you, because that is exactly what Scripture commands and promises. Build the altar. Find an intentional place to lay your hands on the sick and anoint them with oil. Offer that prayer by faith and believe God will do what He said He will do.

There will be times when the presence of God will be overwhelming and your faith will be supernaturally emboldened. But there will also be times when you will pray for people when you have nothing more than your authority and the promises of God to stand on. Pray for them both times. Do it by passion and do it by duty. Keep creating opportunities for your people to experience the power of God and to be healed.

But I must also offer you a warning and a few important considerations. First, elders who do not have their own regular place of prayer will be no more effective than those nine disciples who could not cast out the evil spirit from the possessed boy (see Matthew 17:14–20). Your position only gives you so much authority. You must be living a life of submission as well. You must be praying and building all the personal altars we have previously discussed. It is a hard truth, but it is one I believe to be critically true. Your spiritual life has an impact on the health and wellness of the people you lead. When you have a place of prayer and your church has a place of prayer, the authority that flows through you will be even greater.

Second, there are often elements of God's timing that have an impact on the way that He moves. How long had the blind man sat by that road without sight? Scripture tells us it had been his whole life (see John 9:1–3). Jesus' disciples debated if his blindness had been the consequence of his parents' sins or his own, but Jesus explained he had suffered with blindness so that when he was healed, Jesus' glory would be made even greater. All those years that the man had suffered made his healing an even more compelling witness of Jesus' power.

In another story, one of the greatest moments of evangelism recorded in Scripture came after the healing of a lame man who had suffered from his lameness for years (see Acts

3:1–8). God often uses time—not to deny healing, but to intensify its power and witness.

That means that sometimes we carry our sickness for longer than we would like. We must remember, we are never healed for exclusively physical reasons. God by His wisdom heals so that we might grow in faith and so that His message might be declared to the world. We trust His timing, believing that any time spent waiting serves only to increase the power of our healing and the demonstration of His glory.

> Sometimes waiting looks like soaring. Sometimes it looks like running. Sometimes it looks like walking.

Do you remember Isaiah's promise that those who wait on the Lord will renew their strength? Isaiah described waiting with three images. "They will soar on wings like eagles; they will run and not grow weary, they will walk and not be faint" (Isaiah 40:31).

Sometimes waiting looks like soaring. Sometimes it looks like running. Sometimes it looks like walking. At times, God gives us things in an instant, as the eagle soars and glides effortlessly on the rising currents of air. But at other times, God asks us to run. Do not worry—He promises we won't grow weary doing it, but it will take more time. God often uses our sickness to place us on a track and move us to a position we would not be in without that suffering. We often encounter people that God touches and ministers to through our endurance.

Still, some of us are asked to walk. We are asked to endure for a season, but we do not faint from it. God walks with us.

He uses that season to shape us and to take us deeper into our relationship with Him. Sometimes God is doing something bigger than healing. Sometimes He is doing something bigger than our sickness.

It is not failure if you pray for a person's healing and God chooses to wait; however, it is failure if you stop praying for healing out of fear that people might not get healed. You have not been asked to make those decisions nor give an account for how God chooses to move. You have been asked to lay hands on and pray for those who are sick. Do it by faith. That faith never comes back void. Whether it is an instant moment of healing or the stamina and endurance that allows a believer to shine with brilliant grace through suffering, God is always at work.

You need only to build the altar. Find the place. Show up. Lay hands on people and anoint them with oil as an act of submission to God. Operate in the authority you've been given. Pray. And watch as God's power is put on display for all to see. God is present to heal. We need only to make the space for Him to do it.

The Holy Spirit's gift of healing can pour through any Spirit-filled believer at any time. The ministry of the Holy Spirit is not only given to the leadership of the church, but He is also offered to the whole church. He can flow in His gift of healing through any of the Lord's followers anywhere, not just at a church building or during a church service. He can heal at work, school, or the grocery store. But if we do not have a miracle altar at church, how will those in attendance know how or have the faith to build one in the world

117

outside of their church? Leaders establish an example and an expectation for their followers. If leaders build a miracle altar, so will their members!

### Building the Altar

"Jesus replied, 'What is impossible with man is possible with God'" (Luke 18:27).

1. **Lay hands on the sick.** When it comes to healing, there are few biblical directives clearer than the command to lay hands on those who are sick, anoint them with oil, and offer a prayer for their healing by faith. Do not neglect this work. Perhaps we do not see more miracles simply because we do not do what God has instructed us to do. Find a place to regularly practice the laying on of hands in prayer.

2. **Make room in your life and in your services for the miraculous.** Most of us need structure and order in our daily routines. We need calendars and schedules that keep us on track. But our plans can distract from what God wants to do. We need to be just as intentional about making space for the Spirit to move. We need to learn to wait and give space for the miraculous. We do this by being intentional. Carve out time in your life to wait upon the Lord. Make space in your services for God to move and demonstrate His power.

Never let your plans get in the way of what God wants to do.

3. **Build your faith on the promises of Scripture.** Our expectation of the miraculous is not based on wishing. God has promised to do signs and wonders. He has promised to pour out His Spirit. Make a list of the promises God has made. Find them in the Bible and write them down. Call upon the promises of God when you pray. Allow His promises to build your faith and expectations.

4. **Share testimonials of how God is at work.** I love hearing stories of God's miracles. They move me to pray and believe for more. Testimonials have long been a part of the church's life, and that practice needs to be recovered. When God does something, don't be afraid to talk about it. Invite church members to share their testimonies of the miraculous work of God in their lives. These stories will build the faith of your church and move you to pray for even greater miracles.

# EIGHT

## Building the Salvation Altar

*The same Lord is Lord of all and richly blesses all who call on him, for, "Everyone who calls on the name of the Lord will be saved."*

*Romans 10:12–13*

Every altar, every page of this book, every word and prayer we've shared so far has been leading to this moment. God calls us to repent. He calls us to abandon our way, confess with our mouths that Jesus is Lord, and believe in our hearts that God raised Him from the dead. He calls us to preach His Gospel and build an altar for the salvation of others. Everything leads to that moment of decision. Each altar points to the altar of salvation.

Consider Jesus' first followers. Peter, having walked with Jesus, having witnessed His miracles and teaching, having watched Him die and then be raised to life, having eaten with Him after His resurrection, having watched Him ascend to heaven, and having received the power of His Holy Spirit poured out on them, stood before a crowded street and declared that Jesus was both Lord and Messiah (see Acts 2:5–36). Everything he had seen and experienced culminated into that moment of clarity, that moment of public proclamation. It had all built toward that moment when the Church took up its new work.

**Each altar points to the altar of salvation.**

They built an altar and called the world to repent and receive Christ. They called the world to an altar of salvation. Acts records, "When the people heard this, they were cut to the heart and said to Peter and the other apostles, 'Brothers, what shall we do?'" (Acts 2:37). Peter knew exactly what they should do. "Repent and be baptized, every one of you, in the name of Jesus Christ for the forgiveness of your sins" (verse 38).

That is why Jesus came. That's why His Spirit was poured out. That's why the Church experienced miraculous signs and wonders. That's why they had been praying. Everything had been about that new possibility of salvation. Peter, filled with a new Holy Spirit boldness, called them to repent. It is a message that has echoed throughout time and reached the farthest corners of the globe. We are in on it, too.

We have been called to preach the Gospel and to make disciples. Every altar we build is a preparation for an altar of salvation. Each moment of prayer crescendos into an opportunity for others to receive Christ. We do not pray simply for our own benefit. We pray so that God might move and the Church might be built. Our prayers make way for others to pray their own prayers of repentance. But this altar of salvation depends on us making an intentional space for others to receive Christ. As Paul explained, "How, then, can they call on the one they have not believed in? And how can they believe in the one of whom they have not heard? And how can they hear without someone preaching to them?" (Romans 10:14).

What have we gained if Christ is not proclaimed? What have all our prayers and miracles accomplished if we do not call others to repent and receive Christ? Did Jesus come only to pass out bread and fish? Did He come only to heal broken bodies? Was Jesus sent only to hand out advice for a better life? No, He came preaching a new Kingdom. He came declaring salvation and invited people to follow Him. Peter had it right. Christ came that we might repent and believe. He came so that souls might be saved for eternity. Everything leads to that moment of decision.

We cannot neglect the altar of salvation. If you and your church work diligently to build each of the altars I have previously described and yet fail to create this final place where people meet Jesus, you've missed everything. Your work has been in vain. Worse, you've risked turning prayer into self-obsession.

All the work we have been doing has been a preparation for what God wants to do through us. We have set the table.

We have prepared all the ingredients. We have placed the utensils and carefully folded the napkins. All the food is set out at the center of the table. The feast is prepared, but we've neglected to invite anyone to the meal. What good is all that preparation if there is no one to enjoy it? The food grows cold and spoils. Eventually it begins to stink. So, too, any church that fails to invite others to the feast risks all the preparations rotting and stinking the place up. We cannot neglect the invitation.

## Each Altar Leads to This Altar

Think back through each of the previous chapters. Why do we build our personal altar of prayer? We do it so that we might practice repentance and offer our lives in service to God. Why do we build a core altar of prayer? So that others might join us in supporting the work of ministry and empowering the preaching of the Gospel through prayer. Why do we build a community prayer altar? So that we might pray not only for one another but so that we move the Kingdom forward into the world's darkness. And why do we build an altar for miracles? So that the preaching of the Gospel might be confirmed by signs and wonders.

Each altar exists so that the Gospel might be preached, supported, and empowered. Each altar exists so that the message of salvation might be clearly presented to the world. Each altar exists so that we will be emboldened to call others to a moment of repentance. Each altar exists so that it might support the altar of salvation.

A good biblical example of how these altars build toward that final work is found in Elijah. I believe Elijah spent much of his time alone in prayer or with his fellow prophets in prayer. As we follow Elijah's ministry, we discover that the word of the Lord came to him again and again. "Then the word of the LORD came to Elijah" (1 Kings 17:2). This demonstrates that Elijah was listening and praying even when no one was watching.

**Anything we assume can be soon forgotten.**

Elijah's prayer life wasn't for his own sake. As a prophet, he stood between God and the nation of Israel. Building upon Elijah's faithfulness in personal prayer, God also called him forward into moments of public prayer and miracles. You can clearly recognize that he had both a private altar of prayer and a public altar of miracles.

On Mount Carmel, Elijah gathered Israel and urged them to watch. Elijah did not need to put on a show like the prophets of Baal. He didn't need to wake God up or earn His attention. Elijah knew God. He lived in constant communion with God. He knew he only needed to ask, and God would respond publicly.

So, Elijah repaired the broken altar. He set twelve stones up, one for each of the tribes of Israel, and he prayed a simple prayer. When he did, fire fell from heaven. When the Israelites witnessed the miracle, they fell prostrate before the Lord and cried out, "The LORD—he is God!" (1 Kings 18:39). It is all in this story: Elijah's private prayers, the miraculous sign, and the moment of national repentance is all connected.

Elijah intentionally created a small altar on which God could manifest His power and where Israel could repent before God. And they did! If we pray, we will have opportunities to present the Gospel, and we will see miracles. And if we are faithful, we will call people to repent, and they will come to know Christ. We will build an altar of salvation, and upon it, lives will be eternally changed, and the Church will be built. Christ has promised it. He will build His Church.

Perhaps of all the altars we have discussed, the altar of salvation is neglected because it is most assumed. We all know we are commanded by Scripture to share our faith. We know that preaching the Gospel is at the heart of the Church's calling. Our work, of course, is leading others to Christ. It sounds so obvious that you might have been tempted to skip this chapter. "Tell me something I don't already know," you might have said to yourself. But perhaps our familiarity with this responsibility has allowed us to grow complacent in the actual work. Anything we assume can be soon forgotten.

### The Most Neglected Altar

In my various leadership roles with the Assemblies of God, I have had the opportunity to visit hundreds of churches and sit through even more services. It seems to me that some churches are offering fewer altar calls and are less focused on calling people to an altar of repentance. We may believe in it, but we don't seem to make it a priority. Pastors have a lot to cover in sermons these days. There are questions about faith, challenges from culture, and false teaching spreading amongst believers. I understand how wide those challenges can be. But all the answers and all the carefully nuanced theological sermons matter very little if pastors don't provide an opportunity for people to repent and receive Christ.

Perhaps we assume that we know our congregations and all the people seated in front of us. But we often assume too much. We never fully know what is going on in a person's life. We never fully know how the Lord is at work convicting and calling them forward. Worse, we risk communicating that salvation is not our priority. Our people assume that what we prioritize in our services is what matters most. If the altar of salvation is not a priority when we meet, our people may neglect it all together.

We can't allow the busyness of our churches or our crowded Sunday service orders to keep us from making room for repentance and salvation. Our priority is to preach the Gospel. If we do that, Christ has promised to build His

> We need to give people the opportunity to receive Christ wherever we are and wherever we go.

Church. That is the pattern of the early Church. They prioritized the preaching of the Word. They prioritized calling their neighbors to repentance. God built the Church. He added to their numbers daily. They didn't neglect the altar of salvation.

Though the altar of salvation should be a consistent feature of our time together in worship, I believe this altar must be more prominent than only the occasional concluding moment of some Sunday morning services. We need to

127

give people the opportunity to receive Christ wherever we are and wherever we go. If you look at Israel's moments of repentance, they weren't always in the temple or in a worship service. God moved on His people, and they responded with repentance in all kinds of settings: mountaintops, valleys, battlefields, and farmlands.

Read the Bible closely and you will find God's people repenting all over the place. Everywhere they went, they

**When the Spirit creates a divine moment, grab whatever stones you can find and build an altar.**

stacked up stones as altars and marked moments of repentance. It is the same in the New Testament. The apostles often preached the Gospel in the synagogues first, but they went on to preach in markets, streets, along the roads, and in rented lecture halls. As Jesus' parable once put it, we are to

go into the highways and byways and compel them to come in. The Church has never waited for people to come in to hear the Gospel. The Church has always gone out to them. The Church has built altars in homes, in workplaces, and on street corners and backyards. Wherever the Gospel is preached, there should always be an altar for salvation.

As the old adage puts it, we should always be ready to strike while the iron is hot. I encourage pastors to build this altar of salvation at every possible event: midweek ministries, youth services, fun nights, small groups, barbeques, and block parties. Build this altar both within the church and outside of it. Work this altar into services as well as everyday conversations. And always be ready to abandon your plans when a moment is presented. When the Spirit creates a divine moment, grab whatever stones you can find and build and altar.

One Sunday, as I was wrapping up our opening worship, a person in the congregation began to speak loudly in tongues. Our church, which often experienced the public expression of Pentecostal gifts, grew quiet. We waited and prayed for discernment, wondering if what we heard was meant to be a personal moment of worship or if it was a message to the whole congregation.

When a person feels the Spirit leading them to speak out in words they don't understand, it is often what the Bible calls a message in tongues. "To another speaking in different kinds of tongues, and to still another the interpretation of tongues" (1 Corinthians 12:10). When words in a Spirit-inspired unknown language are spoken publicly as a statement from the Spirit, our response is to listen with our spirit and wait for the Spirit to offer a public interpretation. As I listened to that worshiper's message in tongues grow louder and bolder, I sensed the Spirit was giving me the interpretation.

Often when I sense God giving me the public response, I don't know the entirety of what He wishes to say. God gives me the beginning and I speak by faith as He continues to offer His words. As I began to give the interpretation, I felt the Spirit leading me to speak to a single person who was planning to commit suicide. I spoke what I heard the Spirit saying.

"I know you," I heard God say. "And I know the plan you have to end your earthly life. I want you to know this morning that I have a better plan for you if you are willing to trust completely in Me. I promise to repair your broken life and give you eternal life, if you will accept it."

I didn't have to think very hard or long about what to do next. I gave an altar call. I made an opportunity for the person to respond. Really, it was the Spirit who had made the moment. God had prepared this heart to respond. He had made the moment "hot" for salvation. My job was to present the altar, the space for that person to respond.

Almost immediately, I saw a hand go up in the back row. And just as quickly a person began to move across their row and come forward down the aisle. She was well-dressed and appeared to have her life together; however, inside she was desperate enough to be seriously contemplating suicide. How easily we make assumptions about people without knowing the true state of their hearts.

As I watched her make her way forward, I began to see other people moving as well. Others were responding. In a moment, several were standing at the altar, and many received Christ for the first time that morning. It was a very special Sunday that many of us still remember.

Later, I had a chance to speak with the woman who had first responded to that call. She explained that she had made up her mind to attend church one last time before ending her life. If something meaningful had not happened or changed her, she had been determined to make it the end. God did something that day—but He went on to do more. He changed her and reworked her whole life. She continued to follow the Lord, and God has fulfilled His promise to give her a new life.

She did not get saved that day because of a special segment of service we had predesigned for that purpose. We didn't have a chance to present Christ over a series of social events and get-togethers. She was coming one last time. That was our one and only chance. Because our church had been focused on praying for the miraculous, God moved and did a miracle. God spoke directly to her. And we prepared to stop the service and provide her the altar where she could receive Christ.

Who knows how many people sit in our services facing moments just as desperate. Who knows what they walk in carrying and what decisions they have already made. Who knows if that one Sunday will be the only chance we get. If we are not sensitive to every move of the Spirit, it might be too late. They may leave still lost and hurting. They may never come back. Worse, they might not get another chance.

> We must be willing to pray. There is no shortcut.

When the Spirit moves, He should know that we are willing to listen and willing to respond. God can count on us to build an altar of salvation. But it doesn't take a miracle. Wherever people encounter us, they should encounter Christ. They should encounter an opportunity to receive Christ. Everywhere we go, we build altars of salvation. As we pray and as we teach our people to pray, I believe we will see more miracles. With those miracles, we will see a revival of repentance.

We must be willing to pray. There is no shortcut. What we do in private prayer, like all the altars we have listed, has a profound impact on the public witness of the Church and the public preaching of the Gospel. Each altar builds toward that decisive moment in which a lost soul comes to know Christ. There is no greater miracle than the moment of repentance, salvation, and divine regeneration. Our altars become another person's personal altar to receive the miracle of salvation through the prayer of repentance. That altar is where we welcome God to earth and new believers into our larger ministry of prayer. They begin to build their own altars, which in turn contributes to even more people coming to know Christ.

## Always Be Ready

So, how can we begin to be more intentional about building this altar of salvation? As pastors, we should model the call to repentance in every service so that our congregants learn to do the same everywhere they share their faith. Often our sermons create the opportunities. At the end of your message, offer the congregation a chance to respond.

For some, it might be their first prayer of repentance, but for others, God may be calling for them to renew their commitment to Christ. We will never know if we don't give them that opportunity. Even when your sermon doesn't naturally conclude with a clear call to salvation, there are still ways to provide the opportunity.

Over the years of preaching, I worked out three repeatable ways of presenting the Gospel in a short and concise statement. I had these brief explanations ready for whenever an opportunity presented itself. Sometimes I would take a moment after worship to present the Gospel. Sometimes I used one to conclude a service. Those repeated segments allowed people to respond, but they also trained my congregation to do the same. Anyone who sat under my preaching for even a few months heard me make these presentations and would soon have them memorized. By modeling these statements, I was giving my people a chance to learn how to present the Gospel. I was teaching them how to build an altar and lead a friend or neighbor to a moment of repentance.

I titled one of those quick presentations, Who's Your Daddy? Satan became our father when Adam chose to follow him instead of God. From the day Adam took the fruit in obedience to the devil, we have all been born in his sin and doomed to his hell.

> You belong to your father, the devil, and you want to carry out your father's desires. He was a murderer from the beginning, not holding to the truth, for there is no truth in him. When he lies, he speaks his native language, for he is a liar and the father of lies.
>
> John 8:44

Hell is the devil's rightful eternal home, and all his children are going with him to be with their father when they die—unless they are born again to a new and better father; our Father who is in heaven. "Jesus replied, 'Very truly I tell you, no one can see the kingdom of God unless they are born again'" (John 3:3).

When we put our faith in Jesus, we are born again into the family of God. We are no longer children of the devil and are no longer headed to his eternal home. Now we are headed to heaven, the eternal home of our new Father, God! If you are in need of a new father, meet me at this altar.

Another presentation I gave was titled, Why a Tree? "When the woman saw that the fruit of the tree was good for food and pleasing to the eye, and also desirable for gaining wisdom, she took some and ate it. She also gave some to her husband, who was with her, and he ate it" (Genesis 3:6). It all started at a tree. The Tree of Knowledge was forbidden. They were told not to eat of it. When man disobeyed God and ate of the fruit of the tree, he fell into sin and death. Later God would say:

> If a man has committed a crime punishable by death and he is put to death, and you hang him on a tree, his body shall not remain all night on the tree, but you shall bury him the same day, for a hanged man is cursed by God. You shall not defile your land that the LORD your God is giving you for an inheritance.
>
> Deuteronomy 21:22–23 ESV

Paul said it this way: "Christ redeemed us from the curse of the law by becoming a curse for us—for it is written, 'Cursed is everyone who is hanged on a tree'" (Galatians 3:13 ESV). The curse of sin and death began at a tree and was defeated at a tree. When we put our faith in what Jesus did at the cross made from a tree, we go back to the point of initial sin and begin again, but this time without sin. By the cross we are justified and made as if we never sinned! If you are ready for a completely new beginning, come to the cross.

Finally, I would sometimes use what I call, Why Faith and Declaration?

> But what does it say? "The word is near you; it is in your mouth and in your heart," that is, the message concerning faith that we proclaim: If you declare with your mouth, "Jesus is Lord," and believe in your heart that God raised him from the dead, you will be saved.
>
> Romans 10:8–9

All God asks of us is that we believe in Him and trust Him. The writer of Hebrews says that without faith, it is impossible to please God; therefore, when we put our faith in Him, it pleases Him. Adam did not believe Him. He believed the devil who tempted him, and as a result, he fell from his place with God. He proved his unbelief when he ate the fruit with his mouth. Now in order for us to undo what Adam did to us by his unbelief, we must believe in our heart and put our faith and trust back in God by Jesus' sacrifice, and we must use our mouth to confess our belief. If you are ready to undo what Adam did to you, if you believe in Jesus and are ready to be restored to God, then join me at this altar of declaration.

It wasn't long before people started using these presentations. People would catch me on Sundays and tell me

135

about how they had used one of my Gospel presentations to lead a coworker to Christ. They had the joy of sharing in the work of ministry and the growing confidence that they could share their faith in a compelling and honest way. So, the Gospel began to spread, not only in our church services, but also through the everyday conversations of our church.

For that to work, we have to prioritize and model our Gospel presentation. If we are hesitant to call people to repentance, if we are reluctant to work it into our services, we shouldn't be surprised when our people neglect it in their lives. As pastors, we model it first. We teach our people to do the work of ministry by being willing to do it ourselves.

In the end, we are not giving them work to do but joy to participate in. All of heaven rejoices when a single lost soul is found. We celebrate, too. It is one of the great joys of following Christ. We get to share Him with others. It is also one of the strongest motivators to pray. When your church begins to see miracles and witness their friends and family coming to Christ, their faith is built, their vision inspired, and they are inevitably moved to pray for more.

Prayer was never meant to be a lifeless duty. It was never meant to be about only us. It is a way of joining God in doing the impossible. It is a participation in the miraculous. It is a way of changing the world. And it is one of the greatest joys possible. When we commit ourselves to prayer, lives will be forever changed. Prayer always leads to an altar of salvation.

### Building the Altar

"Everyone who calls on the name of the Lord will be saved" (Romans 10:13).

1. **Learn how to naturally present the Gospel.** I recommend you either develop a few simple Gospel presentations of your own or use mine. Knowing how you can easily transition a service or conversation into a Gospel presentation is key to taking advantage of every opportunity. Having these simple Gospel presentations memorized will build your confidence and empower you to share the Gospel more often.

2. **Be sensitive to the Spirit's leading.** Just as we learn to wait on the Lord and expect miracles, the Spirit will often prompt us to present the Gospel. He knows the condition of each person's heart, and He knows the right moment to call them to repentance. Pray that the Spirit will direct you to these divine moments. Learn to be sensitive to the Spirit's leading, and always be willing to interrupt your plans to state the Gospel and create an altar of salvation.

3. **Take time to invite people to receive Christ.** I believe that every service should provide an opportunity for the lost to repent and receive salvation. That means we must be intentional. It doesn't mean that invitation must come at the end of a sermon. Often it does, but I have called people to salvation during the praise and worship part of our service as well as

during announcements. What matters is that you regularly create places to do it. Don't neglect this most critical work.

4. **Invite those who receive Christ to begin praying.** It is a full circle. Our prayers create the spiritual atmosphere in which God draws a new believer to Himself. That new believer begins his or her walk with God by prayer. Often new believers possess remarkable faith. A part of discipleship should be teaching them how to pray and inviting them into the prayer life of the church. Prayer is one of the beginning and sustaining acts of following Christ.

# NINE

# Our Prayers Accumulate in Heaven

*The four living creatures and the twenty-four elders fell down before the Lamb. Each one had a harp and they were holding golden bowls full of incense, which are the prayers of God's people.*

*Revelation 5:8*

Having described the five altars of prayer, I want to offer a final encouragement. We cannot allow these altars to become another church program. A prayer ministry is not an organizational flow chart. It is not an item on your church's to-do list. These altars have their full effect only when they facilitate genuine prayers of faith. We cannot delegate prayer, and we cannot allow it to become routine. Prayer must build our faith, and faith must move us to more and deeper prayer.

In my experience, the greatest threat to genuine prayer is time. We struggle to make time for prayer, or as time passes, our faith wanes and we lose hope. We grow weary and give up. We are tempted to believe prayer doesn't work, and we gradually lose interest and momentum. If you and your church are going to sustain prayer, if you are going to experience its full effect, you're going to have to pray with endurance. To do that, you need to better understand how our prayers fit into the plans and timing of God. With the right perspective, you'll recognize how passing time doesn't reduce your prayers but allows them to accumulate into something even more powerful.

**Before the throne, our prayers accumulate.**

When God gave me a vision of His throne room, one of the realizations I received that had the most impact was how our prayers exist beyond time. We tend to think of prayers as abstract things. They do not exist in physical space; therefore, we're tempted to think they aren't real. The moment we speak them, they seem gone. But that is not how prayer works in heaven. Before the throne, our prayers accumulate. Our prayers continue to exist after we have prayed them. Our prayers outlive us. They rise to heaven and exist before God until the time of His choosing. When you understand this, it changes the way you pray. It builds your endurance to continue praying.

It is easy to feel as if our prayers aren't being heard. It is easy to feel as if we are tossing wishes up to heaven and hoping something about them will finally move God. When God does not immediately respond, we can feel as if our time praying may have been wasted. I want to challenge you to see your prayers not as wasted but as accumulating. Every prayer you pray rises to the throne room and continues to exist. God collects those prayers. None of them are ignored or ever wasted. God carefully collects the prayers of His people and, in time, they have their cumulative effect.

God's patience is often hard for us to comprehend. He does not always work within the timelines we imagine. That is true not only of His divine actions but also with His patient endurance of sin. The apostle Paul made this point when he wrote to the church at Rome. They wrongfully imagined that God's patience with wickedness was a sign of His indifference to it. They were stubborn and unrepentant, and worse, they thought the wicked were getting away with it. Where was God's judgment?

You might have felt that way, too. Sometimes it feels as if it pays to break the rules and cut corners. But Paul warned that the wicked were storing up God's wrath against them. That wrath would one day be revealed. God does not turn a blind eye to evil. He knows every wrong ever committed. He has record of all the righteous and unrighteous deeds. As Paul went on to explain, God "will repay each person according to what they have done" (Romans 2:6).

No one gets away with anything. God recognizes both the evil and goodness that the world overlooks. But God is patient. Paul described His patience as having a goal. "Do you show contempt for the riches of his kindness, forbearance and patience, not realizing that God's kindness is intended to lead you to repentance?" (Romans 2:4).

Some in Rome assumed that since lightening didn't strike the wicked the moment they sinned, God must not really care. But that wasn't at all what was happening. God was patient. He was at work in ways larger than they could fully comprehend. But He wasn't distant or indifferent.

In the Old Testament, God explained to Israel that their defeat of the Canaanites was not based on their holiness but on the accumulated sin of the Canaanite people. Even as far back as Genesis, God promised Abraham the land, but told him that his possession of it would take time.

**No prayer goes unnoticed.**

God explained, "For the sin of the Amorites has not yet reached its full measure" (Genesis 15:16). The sin of the Canaanites accumulated, and in time it had its full effect; it moved God to act. God had a plan, and His timing was good for His will to be carried out. No sin went unaccounted for.

That is also true of our prayers. No prayer goes unnoticed. No prayer is unaccounted for. Our prayers accumulate, and in God's timing, they also have their full effect. God's patience is always working for that greater good. It is especially true of the way He collects our prayers. John offered a powerful image of these accumulated prayers in the book of Revelation. It is one of the most moving scenes of John's vision of heaven.

John saw a scroll brought forward before God's throne. A voice called out, "Who is worthy to break the seals and open the scroll?" (Revelation 5:2). But no one could break the seals. John began to weep. The scroll contained the plans of God, the plans that had been drawn since before the foundations of the earth, but no one was worthy to open it, nor could anyone understand it. John wept realizing how unworthy he and all creation were.

What John experienced was the same confusion and hopelessness we all experience. God's ways are higher than our ways, and so often we are left confused and perplexed. We struggle to understand the plans and timing of heaven. But one of the elders spoke to John. "Do not weep! See, the Lion of the tribe of Judah, the Root of David, has triumphed. He is able to open the scroll and its seven seals" (verse 5).

John saw the Lamb of God, Jesus, come forward and take up the scroll. As He did, all of heaven fell at His feet. John records, "And when he had taken it, the four living creatures and the twenty-four elders fell down before the Lamb. Each one had a harp and they were holding golden bowls full of incense, which are the prayers of God's people" (verse 8). The elders held massive golden bowls full of our prayers.

How much of human history has built toward that moment when Christ will finally unseal the scroll of God? For all of human history, it has been coming, but it often feels so far off. As the psalmist often prayed, "How long, O LORD?" (Psalm 13:1 ESV). But none of that longing or hoping or praying has been done in vain. As the four living creatures and the twenty-four elders bowed before Jesus, each held a massive golden bowl full of the prayers of God's people. Every prayer for peace, every prayer for justice, every prayer for Christ's return has been accumulating in those bowls. God has collected them all.

Even now, the prayers you pray are placed in those bowls. They are cared for by the stewards of heaven. They are collected and are awaiting that day when they will have their full effect. Your prayers are more than just words, more than abstract wishes. Your prayers are the incense of heaven. They are never wasted. You are never wasting time when you pray them. No, you are filling heaven with them. Sometimes those prayers are answered in our lifetime, but sometimes they outlive us. Sometimes they reside in heaven even after our time on earth. Each prayer has its appointed day in which it will have its full effect. Our prayers move heaven far beyond the moments we pray them.

This is how we remain faithful in prayer. It's how we sustain a ministry of prayer. It's what motivates us to return again and again to the altars of prayer. No prayer is ever wasted. Each prayer we pray is accumulating for that day when God will act upon them. Our prayers fill the golden bowls of heaven. Each day we add more to them. They are the incense of heaven.

### Things You're Still Waiting On

I've often turned to the example of Daniel's prayer life. I am continually struck by his courage and faithfulness in prayer. No law could keep him from it. No risk or threat could make him stop praying. But Daniel must have been tempted at times to give up. So much of what he prayed for never seemed to materialize.

Daniel was stuck in exile, surrounded by pagan idolatry and far from God's Promised Land. He longed to see Israel restored, to see his people return to their land, and to experience worship in God's temple. He prayed for it. Each day, he knelt in his window facing Jerusalem and petitioned God to return them to the land. Daniel was relentless. He explained, "So I turned to the Lord God and pleaded with him in prayer and petition, in fasting, and in sackcloth and ashes" (Daniel 9:3).

Daniel recorded the words of his prayers. They are remarkable. Daniel prayed:

Now, our God, hear the prayers and petitions of your servant. For your sake, Lord, look with favor on your desolate sanctuary. Give ear, our God, and hear; open your eyes and see the desolation of the city that bears your Name. We do not make requests of you because we are righteous, but because of your great mercy. Lord, listen! Lord, forgive! Lord, hear and act! For your sake, my God, do not delay, because your city and your people bear your Name.

Daniel 9:17–19

Daniel did not live to see that prayer fulfilled. God would do it, but Daniel did not live long enough to see it in his own time. Still, his faithful prayers were not wasted. Daniel's prayer was already moving heaven. God gave Daniel a vision of the heavenly war being waged. He was a participant by prayer, but his prayers would not have their full effect until after his life had ended.

Struggling to understand, Daniel prayed for a clearer explanation. God's answer was simple. "Go your way, Daniel, because the words are rolled up and sealed until the time of the end. . . . You will rest, and then at the end of the days you will rise to receive your allotted inheritance" (Daniel 12:9, 13).

It is a hard truth, but if you pay close attention it comes with a remarkable promise. We will not live to see all our prayers fulfilled by God. But the good news is that our prayers outlive us. They continue to work even after we've ceased praying them. Our prayers continue to do their work even after we are gone. What joy we will have when we are with Christ and see those prayers we once long ago prayed still on His mind and fulfilled in their right time. We pray because no prayer is ever wasted. The question is, What would have happened if Daniel had not prayed it through? And what will not happen in the generations to come if we do not pray it through?

> Our prayers continue to do their work even after we are gone.

When I speak or write about the accumulation of prayer, I can't help but think about my grandmother and great-grandmother. My great-grandmother was a godly woman who believed deeply in prayer and longed to see her children come to know the Lord. She carried that burden for decades. My great-grandmother was the first to come to faith, and she took up that work of prayer. When I think of her, I always think of her at prayer.

As a child, my father spent a lot of time at my great-grandmother's house. Every memory he shared with me about her is filled with prayer. He spoke of remembering walking up to the screen door of her house and hearing her praying inside. She was crying out to God, naming all her kids and grandkids. She was petitioning God for our salvation. She did that for years. She prayed and prayed and prayed. Every time he went there, she was praying. She was the most prayerful woman that he and I ever knew. When she died, most of her prayers had not been answered. Most of her family still did not know the Lord. But that had never stopped her from praying.

Years later, as our family gathered to celebrate Christmas, one of my wildest and most lost great-uncles announced to the family that he had given his life to Jesus. We were all shocked—even more so when he explained he had joined a church and was volunteering as a greeter. His decision marked the beginning of a season in our family in which every one of my great-grandmother's children came to know Christ.

My great-grandmother didn't live to see it, but there is no doubt in my mind that our lives were changed because of her prayers. Her prayers worked. They accumulated, and at the right time, when sin had had its full effect, God moved. Our lives were forever changed. My great-grandmother might not have seen all those miracles from earth, but I know she witnessed them in heaven. I believe God spoke to her and said, *"Now is the time. All your prayers have been heard. Join Me and watch as they are answered."* She watched as each of her kids knelt before the Lord and received Jesus. She knew then that none of that time in prayer had been in vain.

I know there are probably things you've been praying about for a long time. You have your own prodigals you name before the throne. You have promises you're still waiting to see fulfilled. Don't stop praying. Keep going. Your prayers are accumulating in heaven. God is collecting them for just the right movement. Your prayers change heaven, they move God. Keep praying with faith. No prayer is ever wasted.

## A Coming Revival

For a long time now, I have been praying for revival in America. I have been praying but still haven't seen it. We need it. Like you, I've witnessed the decline of faith in America and the collapse of moral values. I've watched people walk away from the Church and from Christ. I've seen spiritual apathy setting in amongst congregations, and I've seen our fervor for evangelism grow cold. We need a fresh move of God. We need a fresh outpouring of His Spirit. We need revival. I've been praying about it. I hope you are, too. I won't stop until it is fulfilled or until my time on earth comes to an end.

I do believe revival is coming, but it takes time. God, by His wisdom, is preparing the ground for that harvest. There is specific work that must first be done. Prayer not only helps us usher in that coming revival, but it helps us prepare for it. Why would God bring a revival when the Church is not ready to harvest? Why would God ripen the fruit if the Church doesn't have workers ready to take it from the vine? Before

God can answer our prayer for revival, He must prepare us. He must get His Church ready to receive the lost and disciple them toward Christ. I believe that work is already underway. Prayer is at the center of it.

Before revival can come, God must also do a work in our nation. He must bring about enough brokenness and humility to allow people's eyes to be open to their need. Do you remember the scene of Elijah on Mount Carmel? (see 1 Kings 18:25–29). The prophets of Baal had their own way of calling on their God. Elijah gave them time to demonstrate it, to put their worship and prayer on full display. They cried out to their god who didn't answer. Their prayers grew louder and then longer. Elijah allowed it to play out. He even made suggestions. Perhaps they needed to pray louder still. Perhaps their god was preoccupied or away. The prophets of Baal grew more desperate. They prayed louder and danced harder and eventually turned to cutting themselves. All four hundred prophets gave everything they had. Elijah let them go on from morning until late in the afternoon. Still, Baal did not answer.

For the onlooking Israelites who had long been tempted into Baal worship, the image was clear. Baal couldn't answer. Elijah was wise enough to let the visual sink in. This is what following Baal led to: desperation, exhaustion, mutilation. It didn't work. It never would. Elijah allowed time and space for the consequences to sink in. Finally, it couldn't be ignored.

When the time was right, Elijah stepped forward and prayed a very simple prayer to his God. He didn't need to emulate their desperation. He prepared his altar by restacking the stones and dousing the wood with water. Then he prayed:

> LORD, the God of Abraham, Isaac and Israel, let it be known today that you are God in Israel and that I am your servant and have done all these things at your command. Answer me, LORD, answer me, so these people will know that you, LORD, are God, and that you are turning their hearts back again.
>
> 1 Kings 18:36–37

Immediately, fire fell from heaven and consumed the sacrifice and the altar. When the people saw it, they fell on their faces and cried out, "The LORD—he is God!" (verse 39). They had witnessed the desperation of the world's worship. They had seen its hopelessness. They recognized that Baal would only lead to self-destruction. Their hearts and minds had been prepared to encounter the real, living God. They were prepared for a revival.

**We must sustain prayer for revival through this season.**

I believe we are seeing the same desperate false worship in our world today. Everywhere people are working themselves up, desperate to be healed and restored and to find peace. But they are searching for it by the gods of this age. It isn't working. Every day the self-destruction of the world is made clearer. Every day the hopelessness of this world's idols is put on display. A day is coming when they will not be able to deny the hopelessness, and their hearts will be fully prepared for an encounter with the living God. Even now, God is preparing our nation for that coming revival. Our prayers continue to build it.

We must sustain prayer for revival though this season. We must stay faithful. It is accumulating, and a time is coming when God will say, *Yes! Now is the time*. But like Daniel's faithfulness, like my great-grandmother's, we must continue to pray. We must allow our prayers to accumulate. We must keep petitioning heaven, every prayer being collected. And even if we should not live to see its fullness of time, our prayers are still participating. Our prayers outlive us. And one day, we will witness their fulfilment. Our prayers are building. Our prayers are accumulating.

Keep praying. Pray without ceasing. Do it by faith. Do it for those you love. Do it for this lost world. Do it so that revival might come again. Do it knowing that in the fullness of time, every righteous prayer will be fulfilled.

# TEN

# Control the Altar, Control the Outcome

*If my people, who are called by my name, will humble themselves and pray and seek my face and turn from their wicked ways, then I will hear from heaven, and I will forgive their sin and will heal their land.*

*2 Chronicles 7:14*

God was on His way down to Sodom and Gomorrah. The outcry against the city had become so great that He was determined to intervene (see Genesis 18:20–21). The cities of Sodom and Gomorrah would be destroyed along with everyone in them. But on His way to those cities of sin, God decided to inform Abraham of His intentions. Abraham lived near those two cities, and God took the time to share His plans regarding Sodom and

Gomorrah with Abraham. God had placed Abraham in that land and had promised that his descendants would be great in number. They would fill and inherit that land. So it was that Abraham already bore a responsibility for that place. He was the bearer of God's future plans for that land. In a sense, he was its God-ordained owner.

God's plan to destroy Sodom and Gomorrah was also personal for Abraham. His beloved nephew Lot was living there. Abraham must have understood the risk Lot was in, but it also mattered because God had given Abraham authority over the land. The land was already his by God's promise. It belonged to him and his descendants. We must step into the authority God has given us by taking responsibility for what is ours. Abraham did that by prayer.

You may not realize how much authority God has given you. Certainly, most of Abraham's neighbors didn't consider him an authority. Nobody in Sodom or Gomorrah was paying him any attention. But Abraham's authority was spiritual, not physical. Often spiritual authority and physical authority do exist together. But not always. You do not have to have a physical position of authority to be entrusted with spiritual authority. Abraham had a divine authority because of the promise God had given him. It was his responsibility to remain faithful to that promise and to step into the authority it gave him. It was his job to pray.

As God moved toward Sodom and Gomorrah, Abraham took up that spiritual authority. He went to God in prayer. He prayed boldly. He began to intercede for the few righteous still living in those sinful cities. Abraham prayed, "Will you sweep away the righteous with the wicked? What if there are fifty righteous people in the city?" (Genesis 18:23–24). He continued by prayer to press God for more. "May the Lord not be angry, but let me speak just once more. What if only ten can be found there?" (verse 32). Abraham understood the power of prayer. He understood how much prayer could change circumstances. Through Abraham's intercession, Lot and his daughters were saved.

I believe God warned Abraham so that we might see Abraham's faith and willingness to pray. For Abraham, prayer came immediately. It was his natural reaction. He understood his responsibility. He understood the spiritual authority he carried. He understood that by prayer he could affect the land around him. God warned Abraham so that we might have an image of how a person of faith stewards the responsivity of their altar. It was by Abraham's altar of prayer that he had an impact on the outcome.

> We must step into the authority God has given us by taking responsibility for what is ours.

Abraham wasn't the only one who bore the responsibility of prayer. Consider Moses. When the people turned against God, cast golden idols, and risked God abandoning them, Moses went up the mountain to pray (see Exodus 32). He interceded for the rebellious people, and his prayers preserved their relationship with God. Or consider the prophets whose prayers averted war, revived the people, and broke famines in the land. All of them changed their outcomes by prayer.

All over Scripture, we find believers who are quick to pray. God often found them waiting at their altars. We witness them step into their spiritual authority by taking up the responsibility of prayer. By prayer, they participated in what God was doing. By their altars, they controlled the outcome.

Where will God find us? Where is God most likely to find you? When God moves again through our land, will He find us at our altars? When destruction is upon our land and our nation, will God find us ready to pray? Will He find a people willing to take up the responsibility of the altar? Or will He find us prayerless, distracted, apathetic, lazy, or indifferent?

## If My People

By prayer, God invites us to participate in the outcomes of our world. That is a profound and humbling truth. You need to recognize the responsibility of the authority God has given you. He has called you to lead your family, to honor parents, to love your spouse, to serve a local church, to be a good neighbor to your city, to bless your nation, and to spread the Gospel around the world.

Whenever God calls you to do something, He gives you the authority to do it. You must accept the fact that you play a role in the outcome of your family, your church, your city, and the world. You bear responsibility for it. The future of all you are responsible for is determined at the altar. It is determined by your willingness to go there and pray. You and I are called to pray. When we neglect to build altars and to dedicate ourselves to prayer, we forfeit participation in the outcomes of the world around us. And if we have not manned our altar, we cannot complain about the outcome.

Do you remember the scene from 2 Chronicles when Solomon dedicated the temple? The whole nation gathered, and God's presence descended into the space. God also made them a promise.

> If my people, who are called by my name, will humble themselves and pray and seek my face and turn from their wicked ways, then I will hear from heaven, and I will forgive their sin and will heal their land. Now my eyes will be open and my ears attentive to the prayers offered in this place.
>
> 2 Chronicles 7:14–15

That word was not given exclusively to Solomon or a high priest. God made that promise to the people. God promised to listen to the prayers of all His people. And if any child of God, great or small, humbles themselves, seeks His face, turns away from wickedness, and prays, God promises to listen. God promises to heal their land. He will protect them and keep them. They need only pray.

**Whenever God calls you to do something, He gives you the authority to do it.**

I want to encourage you to take that responsibility seriously. You can start small. Pray and ask God to reveal where He has given you authority. Perhaps your authority is currently focused

157

on your home and the few neighbors around you. That's enough. Take that responsibility seriously. And remember, it isn't about possessing a title. It is about an authority received by the call of God. Build an altar and start praying for your children. Start praying for your spouse. Start praying for your neighbors.

In the gospel of Matthew, Jesus promised that if we can be trusted with a few things, we will be made rulers over many (see Matthew 25:23). It may very well be that your faithfulness to pray for those things closest to you will grow your spiritual authority and God will give you even greater influence through prayer. I genuinely believe that if we can be faithful to pray for our families, churches, and neighborhoods, God will give us the nations. He will heal our land and, by our intercession, reach the world. But you must be faithful with what is before you now.

Remember, it will not always be easy. Prayer is war. When you pray, you enter the conflict of the spiritual world. The devil does not let go easily. There are things that prayer alone can release. This is a theme I have tried to remind you of throughout this book. When you really begin to pray, you will face opposition. But He who is in you is greater than he who is in the world. Prayer is the better weapon. The devil will never win when we pray. He only wins when he can distract us from praying. He wins when he tempts us to neglect the altar. When he can keep us from prayer, from these altars, his authority and power increases. When we pray, when we return to the altar, he loses ground. Whoever controls the altar controls the outcome.

## Do Not Grow Weary

Whatever you do, keep praying. Keep interceding. Keep returning to your altar. Do not let yourself grow discouraged. Your prayers are accumulating. Your prayers are moving heaven. Your prayers are engaging the spiritual enemies of God and unleashing a heavenly army. When you pray, you are building something. You are accomplishing something.

When prayerless people die, everything dies with them. They have only what they were able to accomplish in their own strength. But when people of prayer die, death itself cannot silence them. Their prayers live on. When you pray, you are achieving things you can't yet recognize or foresee.

Daniel didn't live to see his people return to the land, but his prayers helped bring that restoration about. Moses never made it to the Promised Land, but it was his intercession that allowed the rest of the nation to make it. My great-grandmother never saw her children come to salvation, but they are all with her in heaven.

So keep praying. Keep trusting. Keep showing up. Keep building altars and praying forward God's Kingdom. Elijah saw the rain coming even when it was a single cloud the size of a man's hand (see 1 Kings 18:44). By prayer, he knew it was more. The drought would end. Rain was coming.

## Do Not Lose Your Focus

Do not let yourself lose the focus of prayer. It is by prayer that God's people have always lived and died. "They did not receive the things promised; they only saw them and

159

welcomed them from a distance" (Hebrews 11:13). They prayed even as they were tested and as they strained to see the results. They held on to faith by prayer. Prayer has always been at the center of following and obeying God.

Noah, fresh off the ark, built an altar even before he built his own shelter (see Genesis 8:20). Moses did not wait until he reached the Promised Land. He built an altar, a tent of meeting, even as they wandered through the wilderness (see Exodus 33:7). Gideon prayed when he was unsure (see Judges 6:36–40). David prayed when he failed (see 1 Samuel 12:15–17). Hezekiah prayed when the enemy surrounded (see 2 Chronicles 32:20). Josiah renewed the covenant by prayer (see 2 Kings 23). Elijah rebuilt the altar on Mount Carmel (see 1 Kings 18:31–32). Ezra rebuilt the altar in Jerusalem even before he rebuilt the temple (see Ezra 3:2). Jesus recognized that the heart of that temple had always been prayer. He reminded Israel that it was to be a house of prayer (see Matthew 21:13). For God's people, prayer has always been the priority.

Prayer always comes first. Each of these men rebuilt the altar of prayer as their first priority. It is easy to do all that we can in our own strength and then turn to prayer. But that is not the way of God's people. We pray first. It is the first priority. It is what we do most naturally and most often. Rebuild the altar and pray.

## Let's Pray

There is a great danger in talking too much about prayer. Talking about prayer can keep you from actually doing it.

A book on prayer is no replacement for praying. You don't change the world by knowing about prayer. You change the world by praying. At some point, you have to do it. It has to happen. Too much depends on it. Tomorrow longs for today's prayers to be given.

Step into the spiritual authority God has given you. Take up that responsibility. Build a personal altar and start praying. Develop a core team of prayer partners to sustain it. Build a community of prayer through which you lead others. Pray for the miraculous. Build an altar of salvation. Pray and watch God move. Everything depends on it. Whoever controls the altar controls the outcomes.

When God does come, let Him find us at our altars. Let's be praying. Let's do it now.

# APPENDIX

# Building Your Altars

I've compiled for your convenience the application sections from the chapters that discuss the personal altar, core altar, community altar, miracle altar, and salvation altar. Now that you've heard the Word, I encourage you to also be a doer of the Word by applying these truths into your life (see James 1:22–25). The rains, floods, and winds come upon us all, but those who hear the words of Jesus and do them stand when storms of life come (see Matthew 7:24). The Holy Spirit will lead as you seek to build these altars into your life.

## The Personal Altar

"I rise before dawn and cry for help; I have put my hope in your word" (Psalm 119:147).

1. **Decide when you will pray.** Until prayer makes it into our daily planners, prayer is only a good intention. We all tend to pray when pressure or desperate situations move us to pray, but that isn't a daily altar. Fix an appointment with God and keep it. I suggest making prayer your first priority of the morning. Morning prayer reminds us of our need for Him and invites His blessing upon the rest of our day. So, find a time, put it on the calendar, and show up.

2. **Decide where you will pray.** Look for a place away from others where you won't be easily distracted. Find a place to which you can daily return. Even if you struggle to find an ideal place, don't allow your surroundings to keep you from praying.

3. **Start with the Bible.** The Bible itself reminds us that "in the beginning was the Word" (John 1:1). When a person reads the Bible four or more days a week, it has a greater spiritual impact than any other discipline. The powerful effects of Bible engagement on spiritual growth have been reliably demonstrated across many studies. When you pray, there's no better place to start than with the Word of God.

4. **Keep a journal.** When I go to prayer, I often begin by reading from the Bible. I journal what I hear God saying to me through His Word. That experience moves me to pray through worship and with new requests. The Word of God is active and alive and is a powerful guide to prayer (see 2 Timothy 3:16).

5. **Learn to pray the Lord's Prayer.** The Lord's Prayer is a wonderful prayer prompt. Begin by reading the prayer or reciting it from memory. Then slow down and use each phrase as a prompt to pray. Learn to pray for His Kingdom to come. Learn to pray for daily provisions of bread. Learn to pray for His forgiveness and His way of escape from temptation. You can't go wrong with Jesus' prayer as your guide.

## The Core Altar

"Carry each other's burdens, and in this way you fulfill the law of Christ" (Galatians 6:2).

1. **Identify those around you who are already praying.** We all need others to support us in prayer, but prayer partnership takes intentionality. You are going to have to build the kind of relationships with people who will stand with you in prayer. Begin by looking at the people around you who are already praying. Who do you know that believes in prayer and already has his or her own prayer altar? Identify the people of prayer God has already placed in your life.

2. **Ask them to join you in prayer.** Sometimes, all we need to do is ask. Once you have recognized individuals who are passionate about prayer, ask them if they would be willing to pray with you. Ask them if they would be willing to join you as a partner in prayer. Be intentional about asking them to bear this

165

responsibility with you. The act of asking helps establish accountability and intentionality. Keep a list of people who have agreed to partner with you in prayer.

3. **Share your prayer needs.** Develop a regular rhythm of communicating your prayer needs to those who have committed to praying with you. Use whatever means is convenient for your group, including in person, over the phone, by email, and via group texting by phone or app. Prayer partnership is only as effective as your willingness to share needs and call one another to prayer. Don't wait until an emergency or crisis. Regularly find things you can pray about.

4. **Find a regular time to pray together.** Though you can pray for one another in your personal times of prayer, there is nothing like praying together in person. Video conferencing is another way to meet if gathering in person does not work. Schedule a time once a week or once a month to pray together. Pray for specific needs, but also take time to allow the Spirit to speak to you and lead you in prayer. You can also schedule special prayer times when you need discernment or are facing a unique challenge.

## The Community Altar

"For where two or three are gathered together in my name, there I am with them" (Matthew 18:20).

166

1. **Participate in or begin a regular prayer service.** If your church already has a prayer service, make sure you are faithful to attend. If your church does not meet regularly for prayer, perhaps you could start a prayer gathering. You can start with your prayer partners, and then invite the congregation to join you. Your church needs a regular place and time to come together to pray.

2. **Search the Bible for things to pray about.** One thing that can keep you from praying is not knowing what to pray for. I recommend you keep a list of prayers that you find in the Bible. The Bible is full of the prayers of God's people. Pay attention to what they were praying for. What does the Bible specifically encourage us to pray about? You can use this list of prayers as prompts for leading your prayer service.

3. **Practice praying out loud.** Many people feel intimidated to pray. But like many new things, by practice we become more comfortable. Hearing a church pray out loud builds our faith. It encourages us to lift our own voices to God. As we fill the room with the sounds of prayer, our faith grows. The sound of God's people praying is a mark of a healthy church.

4. **Be open to the Spirit.** One of the Spirit's many gifts is leading our prayers. God will guide us and instruct us on how to pray. The Spirit will lead us to prayers we might not have recognized on our own. Come

prepared with a list of prayer prompts, but always be sensitive to where the Spirit is leading.

## The Miracle Altar

"Jesus replied, 'What is impossible with man is possible with God'" (Luke 18:27).

1. **Lay hands on the sick.** When it comes to healing, there are few biblical directives clearer than the command to lay hands on those who are sick, anoint them with oil, and offer a prayer for their healing by faith. Do not neglect this work. Perhaps we do not see more miracles simply because we do not do what God has instructed us to do. Find a place to regularly practice the laying on of hands in prayer.

2. **Make room in your life and in your services for the miraculous.** Most of us need calendars and schedules that keep us on track. Be just as intentional about making space for the Spirit to move. We need to learn to wait and give space for the miraculous. We do this by being intentional. Carve out time in your life to wait upon the Lord. Make space in your services for God to move and demonstrate His power. Never let your plans get in the way of what God wants to do.

3. **Build your faith on the promises of Scripture.** Our expectation of the miraculous is not based on wishing. God has promised to do signs and wonders. He has promised to pour out His Spirit. Make a list of

the promises God has made. Find them in the Bible and write them down. Call upon the promises of God when you pray. Allow His promises to build your faith and expectations.

4. **Share testimonials of how God is at work.** Testimonials have long been a part of the church's life, and that practice needs to be recovered. When God does something, don't be afraid to talk about it. Invite church members to share their testimonies of the miraculous work of God in their lives. These stories will build the faith of your church and move you to pray for even greater miracles.

## The Salvation Altar

"Everyone who calls on the name of the Lord will be saved" (Romans 10:13).

1. **Learn how to naturally present the Gospel.** I recommend you either develop a few simple Gospel presentations of your own or use mine. Knowing how you can easily transition a service or conversation into a Gospel presentation is key to taking advantage of every opportunity. Having these simple Gospel presentations memorized will build your confidence and empower you to share the Gospel more often.

2. **Be sensitive to the Spirit's leading.** Just as we learn to wait on the Lord and expect miracles, the Spirit will often prompt us to present the Gospel. He knows the

condition of each person's heart, and He knows the right moment to call them to repentance. Pray that the Spirit will direct you to these divine moments. Learn to be sensitive to the Spirit's leading, and always be willing to interrupt your plans to state the Gospel and create an altar of salvation.

3. **Take time to invite people to receive Christ.** I believe that every service should provide an opportunity for the lost to repent and receive salvation. That means we must be intentional. It doesn't mean that invitation must come at the end of a sermon. Often it does, but I have called people to salvation during the praise and worship part of our service as well as during announcements. What matters is that you regularly create places to do it. Don't neglect this most critical work.

4. **Invite those who receive Christ to begin praying.** It is a full circle. Our prayers create the spiritual atmosphere in which God draws a new believer to Himself. That new believer begins his or her walk with God by prayer. Often new believers possess remarkable faith. A part of discipleship should be teaching them how to pray and inviting them into the prayer life of the church. Prayer is one of the beginning and sustaining acts of following Christ.

# DEDICATION AND ACKNOWLEDGMENTS

My life and ministry would not have come to be without the prayers of others. I want to dedicate this book and acknowledge all those who have gone before the Lord on my behalf.

My dad often spoke about my great-grandmother's prayers. Her prayers moved his heart and changed his circumstances. She prayed through times that looked as if her prayers might never be answered. She prayed as her children ran from God. She prayed late into the night and rose to pray early in the morning. She was not a minister or a pastor, but she was a prayer warrior who stormed heaven and lived her life in the throne room from an altar on earth. In the end, she greeted her children into the reality of heaven. She only saw two receive Christ while she was on the earth, but because of her prayer, she has now welcomed all five into heaven. So,

I dedicate this book in part to Elizabeth "Ma" Smith, my great-grandmother who prayed my father into faith so that he could lead me down the same path.

Then there were also the prayers of my mom. She would go into my room, lay on my bed, and claim my life for the Kingdom of God. She would argue with the devil the way the angel of God argued for the body of Moses. She would bind his power against me and declare my freedom from his lies, temptations, and distractions so that I could hear the call of God and follow the drawing of the Holy Spirit into the complete will of God for my life. I dedicate this book in part to my mother, Dorthey Ruth Tapley Dubose, who not only gave me life in the natural but also the supernatural.

Growing up around a house of prayer, my father also became a person of prayer. No one could have known that when he finally surrendered to the drawing of the Holy Spirit to receive Jesus as his Lord and Savior, his salvation would include a call to preach, but it did. All those battles at Ma Smith's altar not only produced a saved grandson but another prayer warrior and a preacher of the Gospel. He would not only pastor an effective church—his favorite term—in Dallas, Texas, but he would later heed the call of the North Texas District of the Assemblies of God to lead their District Missions department and later serve as their district superintendent. What I remember most was his life of prayer. His example in prayer and the result of his prayers is why I would also like to dedicate this book to my father, Rev. Derwood W. Dubose.

Today, my greatest prayer support is my wife. She enters her secret place daily and calls on God to watch over her children, grandchildren, and me. She has prayed for me when I was a local pastor, a district official, and now as a national executive. She has prayed for me as a husband, father, and grandfather. She prays for me as a leader, preacher, and intercessor. I do everything beyond my natural level of ability because she lifts me up in prayer. I dedicate this book to Rita Lynn Stratton DuBose.

Finally, I would like to acknowledge and dedicate this book to all of my Sunday school teachers, Royal Ranger leaders, children's church workers, and youth leaders who prayed for me from their secret place or laid a hand on me and called on Jesus to guide me and keep me. If someone happens to read something in this book that helps them or inspires them, it is because God is answering the prayers of all who have prayed for me. We are all better when someone prays for us. So, to all who have called my name in prayer, I want to say thank you, and I dedicate this book to you.

# NOTES

**Chapter 2 Our Prayers Below**

1. Research Releases in Faith and Christianity, "Silent and Solo: How American Christians Pray," Barna.com, August 15, 2017, https://www.barna.com/research/silent-solo-americans-pray/.

**Chapter 4 Building the Personal Altar**

1. Arnold Cole, Pamela Caudill Ovwigho, "Understanding the Bible Engagement Challenge: Science Evidence for the Power of 4," Center for Bible Engagement, December 2009, https://bttbfiles.com/web/docs/cbe/Scientific_Evidence_for_the_Power_of_4.pdf.

**Chapter 5 Building the Core Altar**

1. Jonathan Edwards, *The Works of President Edwards* (New York: Leavitt, Trow & Co., 1844), 486.

2. Jonathan Edwards, "Personal Narrative," quoted in *Jonathan Edwards*, eds., C. H. Fraust and T. H. Johnson (New York: Hill and Wang, 1962), 61.

3. John Maxwell, *Partners in Prayer* (Nashville: Thomas Nelson, 1996), 7.

4. C. Peter Wagner, *Prayer Shield: How to Intercede for Pastors, Christian Leaders, and Others on the Spiritual Frontlines* (Ventura, CA: Regal Books, 1992), 19.

5. Quoted in Maxwell, *Partners in Prayer*, 7.

**Rick DuBose** was elected assistant general superintendent of the Assemblies of God at the 58th General Council in August 2019 and is a member of the executive leadership team.

Prior to his present position, he served as general treasurer of the Assemblies of God from 2017–19. He served as superintendent of the North Texas District from 2007–17 and assistant district superintendent from 2005–07. DuBose pastored Sachse Assembly of God in North Dallas from 1987–2005. Prior to that, he served a pastorate in Hallsville, Texas, and began his ministry as a youth minister in Mesquite, Texas.

DuBose is co-author of *The Church That Works*. He and his wife, Rita, make their home in Springfield, Missouri, and have two daughters, a son, and eight grandsons.